OHIO Real Estate

State-Specific Sales Review Crammer

14TH EDITION

HONDROS LEARNING™

4140 Executive Parkway

Westerville, Ohio 43081

www.hondroslearning.com

20 19   4 5

978-1-59844-268-7

For more information on, or to purchase, our products, please visit www.hondroslearning.com

TABLE OF CONTENTS

PREFACE

Ohio Real Estate: State-Specific Review Crammer ™

You have completed your real estate pre-licensing coursework. Now what? It is time to begin preparation for the real estate licensing exam. *Ohio Real Estate: State-Specific Review Crammer* focuses on the concepts, subjects, and topics you must know to pass the state portion of the Ohio Real Estate Licensing Exam.

A thorough review of the information presented here along with the knowledge you gained from your pre-licensing education are what you need to pass the exam and begin a rewarding career in real estate.

Crammer highlights include:

- Test-taking techniques to help reduce anxiety by fully preparing you for exam day
- Key terms listings to reinforce the terms that form the basis of many exam questions
- Sample exams on key points to immediately apply what you learned to help you retain the information more easily

Additional Exam Preparation Products from Hondros Learning

- Ohio Real Estate Sales CompuCram® Online Exam-Prep
- Real Estate Vocab Crammer Audio CD and Dictionary
- Real Estate Vocab Crammer Flash Cards
- Real Estate Sales National Crammer Course (textbook included)

Acknowledgments

Hondros Learning™ would like to thank the following expert reviewer for his comments and suggestions:

William A. Thompson
Attorney at Law

Having co-authored and edited over 10 books on Ohio Real Estate Law, Ohio Real Estate Licensing Law, and Ohio Real Estate Sales and Broker Preparatory courses, Mr. Thompson has taught Ohio Real Estate prelicensing and continuing education classes for over 25 years and has lectured numerous times on these subjects to the local Board of Realtors® and other related organizations. He has appeared numerous times before the Ohio Division of Real Estate and the Ohio Real Estate Commission. Mr. Thompson has also received numerous awards for teaching excellence during his tenure at Hondros College.

INTRODUCTION

"**D**o it once, do it right, and never do it again!" That is the philosophy I believe in for everything in life—and preparing for the Real Estate Licensing Exam is no different. If you have taken all your pre-licensing courses and built a strong foundation of real estate knowledge, the *Ohio Real Estate State-Specific Sales Review Crammer*™ book, combined with the Crammer Course and CompuCram® Exam Preparation Software, are all you need to pass the exam! In these, you'll focus on the concepts, subjects, and topics you need to know for the Ohio State-Specific Real Estate Licensing Exam—presented it in the format you'll see on the exam!

Our instruction methods can make a major difference in your exam success, but the choice is yours. While we have the knowledge and experience you need, you have a significant role in making the Ohio Real Estate State-Specific Review Crammer™ materials work for you. We'll give you the necessary skills and concepts to pass the Ohio State-Specific Real Estate Licensing Exam, but it's up to you to follow our directions and guidelines *for the best opportunity for exam success.*

The *Ohio Real Estate State-Specific Sales Review Crammer*™ really works! We have developed, and continually update, our program with the knowledge gained in our 40 years. Our results speak for themselves. Hondros College students, on average, score more than 12% higher on the Ohio Real Estate Licensing Exam than others. The students who take advantage of our CompuCram™ Exam Preparation Software consistently increase their opportunities of passing the exam the first time even more!

Simply put, if you follow the Hondros College plan from start to finish, you'll not only pass the exam but also be on your way to a rewarding career in the real estate industry! The statistic we are most proud of at Hondros College is the high percentage of our graduates still in the business at the end of one year, versus the statewide average for the same statistic—91% vs. 60%! That says a lot about our instructors, our classes, our materials, and our ability to prepare you for the real estate licensing exam. So, let's get to it and see how to do it once, do it right, and never do it again!

—John G. Hondros

Test-Taking Techniques

It has probably been years since you have taken an exam. So, let's review a few test-taking techniques that will easily add between 10 and 15 points to your score. First, you need to have a relaxed attitude toward taking the test. If you study and prepare, you'll do fine. Telling your family, friends, and colleagues you are taking the exam places pressure on you by creating expectations, and worrying about everyone's expectations for success may have the opposite effect on your ability to comfortably, and successfully, complete the exam. Go back and tell everyone you have decided to wait a while before taking the exam. Their expectations will disappear, and the sense of pressure will be gone. Try it; it works!

Here Are Some Other Tips:

1. Test moderators enforce the regulations closely. **NO eating, drinking, or smoking**, and **no breaks**. Calculators must be simple, basic calculators. You are limited to one piece of scrap paper. If you run out of scrap paper, hold it up for a replacement. Listen to the guidelines and follow them closely.

2. When you begin the exam, we suggest you immediately write down the concepts and formulas on your scrap paper. This way, you'll be ready to go when you need them (e.g., capitalization rate formulas).

3. Read the question. Read the question. Read the question. Read the question at least **three times** before you look at the answers. Then, read the answers at least two times before selecting the best one.

   People tend to read the questions quickly. Don't do this since you'll often read it so fast you will fall into the "sounds alike" trap and confuse words, (e.g., grantor versus grantee, gross income versus net income).

   When reading a question, do not jump to conclusions. Most questions will have "loss leaders"—statements that do not relate to anything or answers choices with unfamiliar words that sound like possible answers. Before you choose an answer, be sure you have read the entire question and all answer choices.

4. Do not spend a lot of time on one question. Go through the exam and answer only those questions that you *can answer* for certain. If you're in doubt about an answer, skip the question and go to the next one. It's best to move through the questions you can answer as quickly as possible and return to the others later, if you have time. If you are in doubt about a question, "mark" it, skip it, and move on. At the end of the test, after answering the questions you know, review all marked questions, if you have time. Sometimes other questions in the exam will help you answer a question you are unsure of.

5. Maintain your concentration. You may lose your train of thought because of am ambiguous question. This type of question is one that appears to be poorly written, make no sense, or has more than one correct answer. Getting stuck on one of these can throw you off for a series of questions. When this happens, relax—your mind and your muscles—and skip the question. There may be others of these questions on the exam. If, by chance, you miss these because you guess, it will not cause you to fail. What can cause you to fail the exam is becoming so frustrated that you miss the following questions. Keep your composure. Remember, even if you miss these and no others, you will still pass.

6. If a question on the exam appears to have more than one correct answer, look for the best answer based on the supplied information—not your assumptions.

7. Answer all questions, even if you have to guess. Two of the four answers are often not worth considering. Narrow your choices by process of elimination—weed out the obviously incorrect answers or answers you know are wrong. Pick one of the remaining answers when guessing.

8. Your first answer is usually the right one. Don't change it unless you're sure.

9. Answers with absolutes such as *must*, *always*, *greatest*, *never*, and *has to be* are generally not the correct ones.

10. Be careful of "except" questions. You tend to read these questions too fast and even though you know the correct answer, you will choose the opposite.

Example

1. ***All of the following are examples of a specific lien, EXCEPT:***
   a. property taxes.
   b. judgment.
   c. mechanic's lien.
   d. mortgage.

*The best way to answer these questions is to cover the word **except** or **not** when reading the question.*

Answer: b

11. Watch your time to ensure you budget it wisely, but remember time is ***not*** your enemy. You'll have plenty of time to complete the exam as long as you work consistently. Do not spend 15 minutes on one question to get one point, when you could have answered 10 questions for 10 points.

   If you try to answer every question the first time through, you may end up wasting valuable time on the questions you are unsure of. This will only increase your anxiety level. A good time to recognize this behavior is in the Sales Review Crammer™ course—our test has the same type of questions. If you see this happening, make a concerted effort to answer only the questions you know and can complete quickly. After you've regained your sense of balance, answer the difficult questions. If you have used your time well on our exam, you will be prepared for the real exam.

12. Finally, if you have time to review the questions you skipped, take the time to **read the question completely** again. Then, dissect the question into parts (like clauses and prepositional phrases). This will help you understand what the test is asking. This is true even for math questions. When you cannot determine the answer, and before you guess, ask yourself, "What concept is the test trying to make sure I know?" Ask yourself which answer best illustrates that.

   Keep in mind that the purpose of the exam is to make sure you have the minimum amount of knowledge needed to function in the real estate industry.

13. Above all—**don't panic!** During the exam, you may lose your train of thought. When this occurs, stop and take a moment to relax. Take a deep breath, let your shoulders drop; relax your muscles, and your mind, before proceeding. Remember what you've studied. You know more than you think—just relax enough to let it become clear.

14. Be positive and have confidence in yourself. Starting today, say to anyone who will listen, "I'm going to pass the exam," and *mean it*!

Above all, remember there's only one sure-fire way to pass the exam—*study*! This Crammer™ has been developed with that in mind. Follow our directions exactly. To use this manual effectively and pass the exam, read and follow our guidelines. The next section offers tips on studying effectively.

How To Study

The Basics of Good Study Methods

To give yourself the best chance for success on the real estate sales exam, it's important to follow our instructions.

Once you've completed the pre-licensing course(s), immediately begin studying for the Ohio state-specific sales exam by reading this Crammer™ in its entirety and doing the following:

a) Read *Test-Taking Techniques*, and put these ideas into practice as you take the sample exams at the end of the book. Learn the techniques so they become second nature. This can increase your exam score by at least 10 points.

b) Read the *Ohio Real Estate Sales Exam: Outline and Subjects Covered*. The outline does not necessarily represent the order in which you'll see topics on the test, but it will tell you exactly which subjects are covered on the exam and the percentage of questions you can expect in each area.

c) Read *all* of chapters 2 through 5, and the *Glossary*, and *read it no fewer than 3 times!* If a word is in our glossary, it is in the bank of test questions. More than 70% of the state test questions are simply definitions.

   Know the words in the glossary. When you read the glossary the first time, *mark the terms you don't know*. Read the glossary a second time, focusing on the marked terms. Highlight terms you don't know the second time and repeat this review process.

   There's an added benefit to knowing all the terms in our glossary: **If you do not know what a word means in a test answer, then it is probably NOT the right answer.**

d) As you read all sections of this Crammer™ book the first time, *mark the concepts you don't know.* Read the textbook a second time, focusing only on the marked parts. Highlight concepts you don't know on the second reading and repeat this review process. State-specific law and agency questions are areas often missed on the exam. Also, know the ways you can lose your license. **Read, review, and focus on these areas!**

e) There are some charts or graphics designed to help you in certain areas, covering things that have a good chance of appearing on the exam.

f) The exams at the end of the book contain questions similar to those on the Ohio state-specific exam. Grade your exam and review the questions you missed by re-reading those areas in your book.

Golden Rules

If you have studied all the material in this textbook, and followed our advice for test taking and studying, you should do well on the Ohio state-specific sales exam.

To recap the most pertinent points:

1) Read the question. Read the question. Read the question! Read *all* of the answers, too, before you make a choice.

2) Answer all questions, even if you have to guess.

3) Your first answer is usually the right one. Don't change it unless you're sure.

4) Answers with absolutes such as *must, always, greatest, never*, and *has to be* are generally not the correct ones.

5) Know definitions! Study the glossary in this book—if you don't, you are doing yourself a disservice.

6) If you have thoroughly studied the glossary and see an answer on the exam containing a word you don't know, it probably is NOT the right answer.

7) Know the ways you can lose your license.

In conclusion, if you do it once, do it right, and do it as outlined in this book, you'll never have to do it again—and you'll be on the road to success in your real estate career!

About The Real Estate Sales Exam

Application

Before you will be seated for the sales examination, you must complete all required pre-licensing courses. Once completed, send clear copies of your certificates, along with your completed License Application, to the Ohio Division of Real Estate & Professional Licensing. The application must be typed or handwritten in black ink. Any incomplete applications will be returned for correction. To ensure there are no delays in processing your application, make sure everything is complete and included in your application packet. Most importantly, do not forget the $49 application fee. Payment must be in the form of check or money order made payable to the Ohio Division of Real Estate. (The Division does not accept cash.)

Once the Division has reviewed the application and determined eligibility to test, the Division will notify the testing organization (PSI) and it will send eligible candidates an Examination Eligibility Letter and a Candidate Information Bulletin, with instructions for registering and scheduling an exam. Candidates must pass BOTH portions of the real estate sales examination (national principles and state-specific) within one year (12 months) of the initial approval date (listed on the label of your Candidate Information Bulletin from PSI). If you do not pass, you only need to retake the part (or parts) you did not pass. Each time a candidate retakes part of the exam, the candidate must submit a retake application to the Division, with appropriate fee, before a re-examination can be scheduled. If you use the wrong application, you will forfeit your fee and have to submit the correct application with another fee.

Nonresidents of Ohio

Ohio residency is not a requirement to obtain an Ohio real estate license. However, nonresidents are required to file a "consent to service of process" form with their application. This consent permits notice of legal action to be served upon a licensee through the Superintendent of the Ohio Division of Real Estate.

Special Examination Arrangements

In compliance with the *Americans with Disabilities Act* (ADA), applicants with disabilities or those who would otherwise have difficulty taking the examination must complete the Special Arrangement Request form included in the Candidate Information Bulletin and fax it to PSI (702) 932-2666, so appropriate arrangements can be made **before** scheduling the examination. Supporting documentation is also required, including:

- Description of the disability
- Recommended accommodation/modification
- Name, title, telephone number of the medical authority or specialist
- Original signature of the medical authority or specialist

Testing Locations and Dates

Real estate examinations for Ohio are administered only at designated testing centers, located conveniently throughout the state of Ohio. Testing center hours of operation vary depending on candidate demand. They are generally open three to six days a week between the hours of 9:00 a.m. and 5:00 p.m. There will be a toll free number included in the Examination Eligibility Letter sent to all eligible candidates. When calling to schedule an examination, candidates may select the location, date, and time most convenient to them.

Tests are administered at the following locations:

Akron, *Bryden Center,*
1815 West Market Street, Suite 110

Cambridge
1300 Clark Street, Suite #4

Cincinnati
4010 Executive Park Dr., Suite 435

Cleveland, *Interstate Plaza,*
16600 Sprague Road, Suite 85

Columbus South *(Groveport)*
6431 Alum Creek Dr., Suite I

Toledo
1446 S. Reynolds Road, Suite 201

Troy
1100 Wayne Street, Suite 3330

Testing centers are also located throughout the United States. If a candidate wishes to take the test in a different location, they may call 1-800-733-9267. The candidate will need to speak with a Customer Service Representative to schedule outside of Ohio.

Payment of Examination Fees

In addition to the $60 license application fee paid to the Division, there is also an examination fee of either $63 (if taking both the national and state-specific portions at the same time) or $43 (if taking just one portion) payable to the testing service. Payment for examinations is made when registering for the test and scheduling an appointment. If scheduling by Internet, telephone, or fax, you will need a valid MasterCard or VISA. You may also pay by a cashier's check or money order if you register using standard mail. Cash, company checks, and personal checks are NOT accepted. The examination fee is NOT refundable or transferable.

Forfeiture of Fees

Candidates can reschedule an examination for any reason, without penalty, by calling PSI (1-800-733-9267) **at least two business days in advance**. An automated system is available 24 hours a day to cancel and reschedule your appointment. *An important note:* A voice mail message is NOT considered an acceptable form of cancellation. Make sure you use the Internet, automated telephone system, or speak with a Customer Service Representative.

If you cancel your appointment less than two days before your examination date, are late, fail to appear for your examination appointment, or do not present proper identification when you arrive for your examination, your registration will become invalid, you will not be able to take the examination as scheduled, and you will forfeit your examination fee.

Scheduling an Examination

After receiving an Examination Eligibility Letter and Candidate Information Bulletin, you have four options for scheduling your examination. You may schedule *online* (recommended) at PSI's registration Web site (www.psiexams.com). After submitting necessary information, you will be given the available exam dates and locations—select your desired testing date.

You may also schedule over the *telephone* or by *fax*. You may use the automated system or speak with a PSI registrar by calling 1-800-733-9267. You will schedule your examination appointment at that time. You may fax your information (24 hours a day) to PSI (702) 932-2666. After three days, your information should be processed and you can call PSI to schedule your examination. The fourth option is to register through *standard mail*. After mailing in your application, please allow two weeks to process your registration, then you may call PSI to schedule your exam after 7:30 a.m., eastern time, 1-800-733-9267.

The Day of the Exam

On the day of the scheduled examination appointment, it is important that candidates arrive at least **30 minutes prior** to the appointment. Allow plenty of time to arrive at the testing center. You will be held responsible for arriving on time—getting lost, caught in traffic jams, etc., are not acceptable excuses for running late. If you arrive late, you may not be admitted to the examination site and you will forfeit your examination registration fee. If you choose not to take the examination at that time, you must reapply in order to be seated again.

You must provide **two forms of identification** upon arrival at the test site.

One must be a *VALID government-issued photo identification that also bears your signature* (e.g., driver's license, state ID card, passport). The second form of identification *must have your signature and your preprinted legal name.*

All identification must match the name on your Examination Registration form and your Registration Confirmation Notice. If you are unable to provide the required identification, you must call PSI (1-800-733-9267) at least **three weeks prior** to your scheduled appointment to arrange a way to meet this security requirement. *Failure to meet this identification requirement at the time of your examination without notifying PSI is considered a missed appointment and you will NOT be able to take the examination.*

Regulations and Testing Procedures

To ensure that all applicants are tested under equal conditions, the following regulations and procedures are observed at all test centers:

- Weapons of any kind are NOT permitted.

- Candidates may bring a silent, simple (non-programmable) pocket calculator. This means a standard four function (+, -, x, ÷) calculator that is battery operated and non-printing. Calculators with alphanumeric keys are not permitted.

- All examinations are closed book. No notes or reference materials of any kind are permitted.

- No cellular phones, pagers, purses, briefcases, personal belongings, or children are permitted in the examination site.

Dress in loose, comfortable clothing. Wear layers to accommodate for room temperature changes.

Please note that NO EATING, NO DRINKING, NO SMOKING, nor tobacco of any kind is allowed in the examination area. There are also *no* rest breaks once the examination begins, so please plan accordingly.

Computer Testing System

Examinations are administered on a personal computer similar to those in homes and offices. Answers are recorded using a mouse and/or keyboard. The system is very simple to use, even for those with no previous typing or computer experience. Candidates have an opportunity to practice using the system (maximum of 15 minutes) before beginning their exam. The time used for practice is *not* deducted from the actual exam time.

Examination Structure

The Ohio Real Estate Sales Examination consists of two parts: 1. A "national" part focusing on general real estate principles and practices and, 2. A "state-specific" part focusing on Ohio law and practices. First-time candidates must test on both parts (unless the national part has been waived by the Superintendent for a candidate already licensed in another state). Candidates must pass both parts to satisfy the licensure requirements. Candidates who pass only one portion of the test need only retake the portion they failed; however, they must re-apply and retake the failed portion of the exam within one year of the initial Eligibility Letter.

The two portions of the Ohio real estate sales exam are:

1. National part—80 questions, 2 hour time limit
2. State-specific part—40 questions, 1 hour time limit

All test questions are in *multiple-choice format*, with one correct answer and three incorrect options. If you are not sure of the answer to a question, you may "mark" it and move on, so that at the end of the test you can review all marked questions, if time allows. You also have the option of reviewing all of your answers at the end of the test if you have enough time. Each examination may also include five to ten "future test" questions mixed into the test. These questions are not counted as part of the final score and the time used to answer them will not count against your total examination time.

Score Report

As soon as candidates complete their tests, they receive a score report indicating whether they passed or failed. All exam scores are scaled to ensure fairness, so each candidate receives an exam of equal difficulty to all other candidates. A score of at least 70% is required to pass the examination. Candidates must pass both portions of the exam.

The testing service electronically transmits score information to the Division each business day. Candidates who have passed both portions of the test will be issued a license by the Superintendent, which should be completed within three business days. You should wait until your broker actually receives your license from the Division before you begin practicing real estate.

Examination Tips

Before you begin your test, read the directions carefully. Be sure you understand them before attempting to answer any questions.

Once you begin the examination, use your time economically. Answer the questions in order, but do not waste time on those containing unfamiliar material or that are too difficult for you. Proceed to the other questions, and return to the difficult ones later, if you have time.

For each question, you must decide which one of the suggested answers is the most correct. *It is better to attempt to answer a question than not to answer it at all.*

Your score will be based on the number of questions you answer correctly on the examination. Since very few applicants answer all questions correctly; do not be concerned if there are some questions you cannot answer.

Be informed, be prepared, and go to the exam relaxed and ready for success.

One of our goals at Hondros College is to send you to the state sales exam with a complete understanding of what you'll encounter. If you are completely prepared, you are more likely to go to the exam feeling confident and equipped to successfully pass the exam.

Ohio Real Estate Sales Exam: Outline and Subjects Covered

The Ohio Real Estate Sales Exam consists of two parts: 1. A **national portion** (80 questions) that focuses on national principles of real estate practice; 2. A **state portion** (40 questions) that focuses on Ohio real estate law and practice. Also included are questions requiring general knowledge of real estate. The following outline gives some guidance as to the percentage and approximate number of questions covered by each topic on the Ohio state-specific exam.

State Outline—Ohio Law and Practice

I.   State Governance of the Real Estate Profession   **(10%—about 4 questions)**

    A.   General powers and structure of governing bodies

    B.   Audit of records

    C.   Investigations, hearings, and appeals

    D.   Violations and penalties (includes fines, suspension, license revocation, education sanctions, public reprimands)

    E.   Recovery fund

II.   Licensing Requirements   **(15%—about 6 questions)**

    A.   Activities requiring a license

    B.   License renewal and maintenance

    C.   Change in license status (military, retired, inactive)

    D.   Post license education and continuing education

    E.   Eligibility for licensing (Broker only)

III.   License Law and Rules of the
Ohio Real Estate Commission   **(40%—about 16 questions)**

    A.   Advertising/use of business name/misrepresentation/team advertising

    B.   Broker/Salesperson employment or independent contractor agreement

    C.   Commissions and fees paid through broker only/agent compensation

    D.   Document handling and record keeping (includes contracts and listings)

    E.   Handling of monies/considerations (items of value)

    F.   Trust or special accounts

    G.   Types of listings and rules

    H.   Offers, counteroffers, and acceptance

    I.   Ohio broker lien law (broker only)

    J.   Inducements

    K.   Ancillary trustee (procedure if broker dies)

    L.   Property management (includes leases)

M. Rentals

N. Fair housing sign and broker's license display (Broker only)

IV. Brokerage Relationships (Agency Law)   **(35%—14 questions)**

  A. Creating agency and agency contracts/types of agency relationships

  B. Licensee duties and obligations to clients and customers, licensee liabilities, waiver of duties

  C. Termination of agency

  D. Confidentiality

  E. Disclosure of agency relationships and listing information

  F. Disclosures required when dealing with own properties

  G. Unauthorized practice of law

  H. False representations of license status or expertise

  I. Canon of Ethics

Ohio Real Estate License Law: Annotated Version

I n order to be a real estate salesperson or broker, an applicant must meet the requirements of the Ohio Real Estate License Law. Every state has enacted real estate license laws that regulate the activities of brokers and salespeople.

The purpose of the license law is to protect the public from dishonest, incompetent, or unscrupulous real estate agents. It also ensures that all salespeople and brokers meet certain educational and professional requirements.

This chapter contains an overview of the Ohio Revised Code and the Ohio Administrative Code that are relevant to Ohio Real Estate licensing. Should the reader wish to view the actual Statutes and Administrative Code Sections; please refer to Ohio Revised Code Sections 4735.01 to 4735.99 and Ohio Administrative Code Sections 1301: 5-1-01 to 1301: 5-7-04, which can be easily accessed through the Ohio Division of Real Estate website.

Ohio Real Estate Commission A five-member committee that can adopt, amend, or rescind regulations concerning real estate licensing.

Superintendent of the Division of Real Estate The administrator of the Real Estate License Law and the Division of Real Estate.

Real Estate Education and Research Fund A fund created to advance real estate education and research and to provide educational loans to salesperson applicants.

Real Estate Recovery Fund (RERF) Provides funds to compensate injured parties who have obtained a court judgment against an insolvent licensed salesperson or broker.

License Renewal All licensees must renew their own licenses each year on or before their own birthday.

Pre-License and **Post-License Requirements** Education Requirements.

Continuing Education Education required of all salespersons and brokers every three years.

Key Terms

Administration

The Real Estate Law is administered by the Real Estate Commission and the Superintendent of the Division of Real Estate, both of which fall under the domain of the Ohio Department of Commerce.

The Real Estate Commission

The Real Estate Commission is comprised of five members who are appointed to five-year terms by the Governor, with the advice and consent of the Senate. Four of the members must have been engaged in the real estate business as licensed real estate brokers in Ohio for at least ten years immediately preceding appointment to the Commission. The fifth member represents the public (and is not a licensed broker or salesperson). No more than three members of the Commission can be of the same political party.

The Commission:

1. Adopts canons of ethics for the real estate industry.

2. Upon appeal by any party affected, or upon its own motion, may review any order of the Superintendent of the Division of Real Estate, and may reverse, vacate, or modify any order of the Superintendent.

3. Administers the Real Estate Education and Research Fund and hears appeals from orders of the Superintendent regarding claims against that fund or against the Real Estate Recovery Fund.

4. Directs the Superintendent on the content, scheduling, instruction, and offerings of real estate courses for salespersons and broker educational requirements.

5. Distributes to licensees and the public, information relative to Commission activities and decisions.

6. Notifies licensees of changes in state and federal civil rights laws pertaining to discrimination in the purchase or sale of real estate and relevant case law, and informs licensees they are subject to disciplinary action if they don't comply with the changes.

7. Publishes and furnishes to public libraries and to brokers booklets on housing and remedies available to dissatisfied clients.

8. May levy fines up to $2,500 per license law violation, with no limit.

Structure of Ohio Real Estate Regulatory Agencies

Ohio Department of Commerce (Director of Commerce)

Ohio Real Estate Commission

Ohio Division of Real Estate

5 members appointed by Governor with advice and consent of Senate;
Term of office 5 years

4 members licensed at least 10 years as broker;
1 holds no real estate license;
No more than 3 from one political party

Superintendent of Real Estate appointed by Director of Commerce;
3 names suggested by Commission
Term of office: terminated anytime by the Director of Commerce

Duties

1. Investigate complaints and subpoena witnesses
2. Apply to court for injunction or restraining order
3. Promote Canon of Ethics
4. Review decisions of Superintendent
5. Review education requirements
6. Administer REERF* and hear appeals regarding claims against Recovery Fund
7. Distribute information
8. Notify licensees of charges in discrimination laws
9. Publish and distribute booklets on housing and discrimination laws
10. Publish and distribute booklets on housing and remedies for dissatisfied clients
11. Determines and issues penalties: suspension, revocation, fines, continuing education, public reprimand
12. May fine up to $2,500 per license law violation (no limit)

Duties

1. Investigate complaints and subpoena witnesses
2. Apply to court for injunction or restraining order
3. Administer Real Estate License Law
4. Issue orders to implement the law
5. Maintain investigation and audit records of brokers and salespersons
6. Administer the issuance, suspension, and revocation of licenses
7. Appoint hearing examiner and ancillary trustee with approval of probate court
8. Approve or reject brokerage business names
9. Administer Recovery Fund
10. May fine $200 per advertising law violation up to a maximum total of $2,500

The Superintendent of the Division of Real Estate

Also under the Ohio Department of Commerce is the Division of Real Estate. The Director of the Department of Commerce appoints a Superintendent of the Division of Real Estate. Within 60 days after the Office of Superintendent becomes vacant, the Ohio Real Estate Commission submits the names of three persons whom the Commission considers qualified for the position of Superintendent. The Director then chooses the Superintendent from among these three names. The Superintendent's term of office is indefinite. However, the Superintendent serves at the pleasure of the Director. This means that the Director can terminate the Superintendent at will (at any time) without consulting the Commission.

Duties. The Superintendent is the administrator of the Real Estate License Law and may issue any orders of the Commission or any other orders necessary to carry out the provisions of the real estate law. The Superintendent also serves as the Executive Director of the Commission. The State Attorney General is the legal advisor to the Superintendent, represents the Division in complaint and legal cases, and renders legal opinions relating to the Real Estate Law.

Either the Commission or the Superintendent of Real Estate may:

A. Investigate complaints and may subpoena witnesses in connection with investigations. The failure of a licensee to obey a subpoena pertaining to an inquiry or investigation conducted by the Commission or Superintendent may constitute prima facie evidence of misconduct.

B. Make application to the appropriate court for an order enjoining violations or for an injunction, restraining order, or other orders as may be appropriate.

The Superintendent also:

1. Administers the license law.

2. Issues all orders necessary to implement the license law.

3. Investigates complaints concerning violation of the license law or the conduct of any licensee.

4. Establishes and maintains an investigation and audit section to investigate complaints and conduct inspections, audits, and other inquiries appropriate to enforce the license law. The investigators or auditors have the right to review and audit business records of licensees during normal business hours.

5. Appoints a hearing examiner for any proceeding involving license suspension or revocation.

6. Administers the Real Estate Recovery Fund.

7. Approves or rejects brokerage business names.

8. Appoints a trustee. Upon the death of a licensed broker or the revocation or suspension of his license, the Superintendent may appoint, upon application by any interested party, or, in the case of a deceased broker, subject to approval by the probate court, recommend the appointment of an ancillary trustee who is qualified to conclude the business transactions of the deceased, revoked, or suspended broker.

9. May levy fines of $200 per violation of agency, advertising, and fair housing language law, with a maximum total of $2,500.

Who Must Be Licensed?

The Ohio Real Estate Law states that no person, partnership, limited liability partnership, association, corporation, or limited liability company can act as a real estate broker or real estate salesperson, or advertise or assume to act as such, without first being licensed.

Broker. The definition of a real estate broker includes any person, partnership, limited liability partnership, association, corporation, or limited liability company who for another and for a fee, commission or other valuable consideration, or with the intention, or in the expectation, or upon the promise of receiving or collecting a fee, commission, or other valuable consideration, engages in any of the following activities:

1. Sells, exchanges, purchases, rents, or leases, or negotiates the sale, exchange, purchase, rental, or leasing of any real estate.

2. Offers, attempts, or agrees to negotiate the sale, exchange, purchase, rental, or leasing of any real estate.

3. Lists, or offers, attempts, or agrees to list, or auctions, or offers, attempts, or agrees to auction, any real estate.

4. Buys or offers to buy, sells or offers to sell, or otherwise deals in options on real estate.

5. Operates, manages, or rents, or offers or attempts to operate, manage, or rent, other than as custodian, caretaker, or janitor, any building or portions of buildings to the public as tenants.

6. Advertises or holds oneself out as engaged in the business of selling, exchanging, purchasing, renting, or leasing real estate.

7. Directs or assists in the procuring of prospects or the negotiation of any transaction, other than mortgage financing, which does or is calculated to result in the sale, exchange, leasing, or renting of any real estate.

8. Is employed by or on behalf of the owner of lots, or other parcels of real estate, at a stated salary, or upon a commission, or upon a salary and commission basis or otherwise, to sell such real estate, or any parts of it, in lots or other parcels, and who sells, exchanges, or offers, attempts, or agrees to negotiate the sale or exchange of any such lot or parcel of real estate.

9. Is engaged in the business of charging an advance fee or contracting for collection of a fee in connection with any contract whereby the person undertakes primarily to promote the sale, exchange, purchase, rental, or leasing of real estate through its listing in a publication issued primarily for such purpose or for referral of information concerning such real estate to brokers, or both, except that this division does not apply to a publisher of listings or compilations of sales of real estate by their owners.

10. Collects rental information for purposes of referring prospective tenants to rental units or locations of such units and charges the prospective tenants a fee.

Broker
· Sells
· Exchanges
· Purchases
· Rents or leases
· Lists
· Auctions
· Options
· Offers, attempts, or agrees to perform or negotiate one of these activities
· Advertises or holds self out as engaging in any of these activities

Salesperson. A real estate salesperson is defined as any person associated with a licensed real estate broker to do or to deal in any acts or transactions set out or comprehended by the definition of a real estate broker, for compensation or otherwise.

BROKER	SALESPERSON
1. Person, partnership, limited liability partnership, association, limited liability company, or corporation 2. Receives fee, commission or other valuable consideration. 3. Acts for another to sell, exchange, purchase, rent, lease, negotiate, auction, option, operate, or manage real estate	1. Person 2. Associated with licensed real estate broker 3. With or without compensation

Exceptions to Being Licensed. A real estate license is not required of those who perform any of the acts generally included in the definition of a real estate broker, if the action is performed:

1. With reference to real estate owned by a person, partnership, limited liability partnership, association, corporation, or limited liability company, or acquired on his own account in the regular course of, or as an incident to, the management of the property.

2. As receiver or trustee in bankruptcy, as guardian, executor, administrator, trustee, assignee, commissioner, under authority or appointment of any court, or as a public officer, or as executor, trustee, or other bona fide fiduciary under any trust agreement, deed of trust, will, or other instrument creating a similar fiduciary obligation.

3. As a public officer while performing official duties.

4. As an attorney at law in the performance of legal duties.

5. As the sale of manufactured or mobile homes that do not include real estate.

Exceptions—*The following people do NOT require a real estate license:*

1. Property owners **selling their own property** or **regular salaried employees** of an owner in transactions with the owner's own property.
2. Court-appointed **fiduciaries**, (i.e., guardians, executors, receivers, trustees)
3. **Public officials** performing official duties.
4. **Attorneys** in the performance of their legal duties.
5. Persons selling **manufactured** or **mobile homes** that do not include land.
6. Persons selling interests in business assets that does not include the sale of real property.
7. As a person who engages in the sale of commercial real estate pursuant to the requirements of section 4735.022 of the Revised Code.

Foreign Real Estate Dealer. Foreign real estate means real estate not situated in Ohio, and any interest in real estate not situated in Ohio. A foreign real estate dealer is anyone who meets the definition of a real estate broker, but acts with respect to foreign real estate (real estate located outside of Ohio).

Foreign real estate licenses require separate and different applications and examinations. However, if the person seeking a foreign license is currently, and has been, an active Ohio broker for at least two years, the exam may be waived.

Foreign Real Estate Salesperson. A foreign real estate salesperson is any person associated with a licensed foreign real estate dealer to do or deal in any transaction permitted by definition of a foreign real estate dealer, for compensation or otherwise.

Interests in foreign real estate can only be sold or negotiated by foreign real estate licensees.

Example

A newspaper ad in Ohio advertises the sale of a timeshare development in Florida. This sale must be handled by a foreign real estate licensee.

However, owners selling their own foreign real estate in a single transaction are exempt from the foreign licensing requirements.

Example

An Ohio resident owns a condominium in Florida. The owner runs an ad in an Ohio newspaper offering to sell his/her own condominium. The owner is not required to be a broker or to be licensed as a foreign real estate dealer.

Salesperson Pre-License Requirements

The requirements to become a licensed Real Estate Sales Associate are:

1. You must be honest, truthful, and of good reputation.

2. You must be at least 18 years old.

3. You must be sponsored by an Ohio broker in good standing.

4. You must not have been convicted of a felony or crime of moral turpitude, adjudged by a court to have violated any civil rights laws regarding real estate within the past two years, or violated any rules of the Ohio Division of Real Estate. If you have been found to have done so, and at least two years have passed, you must have satisfied the Superintendent that you will not violate such laws or rules again in order to be reinstated.

5. If you were born after 1950, you must have a high school diploma or its equivalent as recognized by the Ohio Department of Education.

6. You must successfully complete at an institute of higher education:

   a. Forty hours (40) of classroom instruction in real estate **principles and practices**.

   b. Forty (40) hours of classroom instruction in Ohio real estate **law**, including civil rights, new case law on housing discrimination and desegregation problems, and methods of eliminating the effects of prior discrimination. If feasible, law instruction should be taught by a member of the faculty of an accredited law school, and if feasible, civil rights instruction should be taught by a staff member of the Ohio Civil Rights Commission. *Note: The course in real estate law is not required of an applicant admitted to practice law before the Supreme Court of Ohio.*

    c. Twenty (20) hours of classroom instruction in real estate **appraisal.**

    d. Twenty (20) hours of classroom instruction in real estate **finance**.

Anyone not licensed as a real estate salesperson or broker within the four years immediately preceding the current application for the salesperson's exam must have completed the required classroom instruction within ten years immediately preceding the current salesperson application.

Example

Sam is 42 years old. He first got his real estate salesperson's license 20 years ago. However, about 12 years ago, he started a new career and let his salesperson license lapse. Now, Sam has decided he wants to get into real estate again. He took a real estate law and a real estate appraisal class 15 years ago. Since Sam was not licensed within the preceding four years, and since it has been more than ten years since he took these classes, they cannot be used in his current application. Sam must re-take the real estate law and real estate appraisal classes, and also take finance and principles and practices classes.

Pre-Licensing Requirements
Total of 120 hours (classroom or online) must be completed at a degree-granting institution covering:
1. Real Estate Principles and Practices (40 hours)
2. Real Estate Law (40 hours)
3. Real Estate Finance (20 hours)
4. Real Estate Appraisal (20 hours)

Nonresidents of Ohio

Ohio residency is not a requirement to obtain an Ohio real estate license. However, non-residents are required to file with their application a consent to service of process, which permits notice of legal action to be served upon them through the Superintendent of the Ohio Division of Real Estate.

Reciprocity

Reciprocity of real estate licensing between states is not considered unless the licensing state has requirements similar to Ohio's. (Current consideration is given to real estate licensees from Arkansas, Colorado, Connecticut, Mississippi, Nebraska, Oklahoma, West Virginia and Wyoming. For the most current updated info, please visit the following website: www.com.state.oh.us/real). These instances should be researched through the Ohio Division of Real Estate and the state authority where the candidate is currently licensed.

Department of Commerce

Division of Real Estate & Professional Licensing

John R. Kasich, Governor   77 South High Street, 20th Floor
David Goodman, Director   Columbus, Ohio 43215-6133 U.S.A.

Please visit our website at
www.com.ohio.gov/real

614 | 466-4100
Fax 614 | 644-0584
TTY/TDD: 800 | 750-0750

SALESPERSON

LICENSE EXAMINATION APPLICATION

FEE: $60.00

- **Incomplete applications and applications that are filled out incorrectly will be returned for correction.**
- Attach a copy of the transcript or certificate of completion of the four required pre-licensure classes.
- A check or money order for **$60.00** made payable to: Division of Real Estate & Professional Licensing, must be remitted with this form. **Cash will not be accepted.**

Note: The name and date of birth on this application must match the name and date of birth on the government issued photo identification you will use to identify yourself at the examination site.

FOR DIVISION USE ONLY
FILE NUMBER

APPLICANT INFORMATION

FIRST NAME	MIDDLE NAME	LAST NAME	SUFFIX
HOME ADDRESS		HOME PHONE ( )	SOCIAL SECURITY NUMBER

CITY	STATE	ZIP CODE + 4	COUNTY	YEAR OF HIGH SCHOOL GRADUATION/G.E.D.	DATE OF BIRTH (mm/dd/yyyy)

EMAIL ADDRESS

BROKER INFORMATION: Enter the information for the company you plan to be associated with below.

COMPANY FILE NUMBER	BROKER/COMPANY NAME	BUSINESS PHONE ( )	BUSINESS FAX ( )
MAIN BUSINESS ADDRESS (NOT A BRANCH OFFICE ADDRESS)	CITY	STATE	ZIP CODE + 4

ETHICAL CONDUCT AND LEGAL HISTORY

- **PLEASE ATTACH A COMPLETE EXPLANATION FOR ANY QUESTIONS ANSWERED "YES" BELOW.**
- QUESTIONS CONCERNING PROFESSIONAL LICENSES APPLY TO ALL PROFESSIONAL LICENSES REGARDLESS OF PROFESSION.

☐ YES ☐ NO Have you ever been disciplined in any manner by any public entity or professional or trade association for any violation of any professional licensing law, regulation or ethical rule?

☐ YES ☐ NO Have you ever been refused or denied any professional license or registration by any public entity?

☐ YES ☐ NO Have you ever had any professional license revoked, suspended or limited in any way for any reason?

☐ YES ☐ NO Have you ever been notified by any public entity or professional or trade association that you were under investigation for any violation of any professional licensing law, regulation or ethical rule?

☐ YES ☐ NO Have you ever been the subject of any unsatisfied judgments?

☐ YES ☐ NO Have you ever been convicted of, plead guilty to or been granted intervention in lieu of conviction for any unlawful conduct excluding minor traffic violations? EXPLAIN:

THE APPLICANT MUST COMPLETE THE FOLLOWING CERTIFICATION

I certify that all of the statements on this application and all of the attached materials are complete and accurate. I understand that any false statement on this form or the attached materials may subject me to criminal prosecution and the loss of my Ohio real estate license.

SIGNATURE OF APPLICANT	DATE

THE SPONSORING BROKER MUST COMPLETE THE FOLLOWING CERTIFICATION

I hereby certify that, from the investigations made by me, I find the above listed applicant for a real estate license is honest, truthful and of good reputation. I understand that any false statement on this form or the attached materials that is known to me at the time of my signing may subject me to criminal prosecution and the loss of my Ohio real estate license.

NAME OF BROKER (please type or print)	FILE NUMBER	SIGNATURE OF BROKER	DATE

NOTICE: Per R.C. Section 149.43, this application and the information contained therein, except for the social security number, is public record.
NOTICE: Per R.C. Section 4735.09(B), if an application is denied prior to the applicant's being admitted to the examination, the division, to cover the expenses of processing the application, shall retain one-half of the fees and the other one-half shall be returned to the applicant.
NOTICE: Refusal of check payment by the drawer's bank my result in a $100 fee to the superintendent and/or the rejection or withdrawal of this application.

COM 3568 (Rev. 02/2010)   *"An Equal Opportunity Employer and Service Provider"*   Page 1 of 1

Licenses

The license of each real estate broker and each salesperson associated with the broker is mailed to the broker. Each license shows the name and address of the licensee and, in the case of partnerships, limited liability partnerships, associations, limited liability companies, and corporation licenses, the name and address of each member or officer. A salesperson's license shows the name of the broker with whom the salesperson is to be associated.

√ **Note:** A salesperson is permitted to engage in the practice of real estate in Ohio when the salesperson's license has been issued by the Division of Real Estate. In the real world, *do NOT* practice real estate until your broker receives your license from Division.

Post-Licensing Requirements

Within one year after becoming licensed, a salesperson is required to successfully complete an additional 20 hours of online or classroom instruction in a real estate course (or courses) that cover current issues regarding consumers, real estate practice, ethics, and real estate law.

If a salesperson does not file proof of having successfully completed these courses within one year, the license will be automatically suspended. The salesperson is then given a one-year grace period following suspension in which to take this instruction. If the 20 hours of instruction are completed within the grace period, the salesperson may request reactivation of the license by filing a reactivation application along with a fee of $49.00. If the request for reactivation is not filed within the one-year grace period, the salesperson's license is automatically revoked. In order to obtain a new license, the person would have to resubmit an application *and* retake the salesperson examination.

Continuing Education (CE)

All active salesperson and broker licensees have continuing education (CE) requirements. Except those licensees who attain 70 years of age, ALL active licensees must complete 30 hours of CE requirements every three years. Of these 30 hours of study, 3 hours must involve legal issues and recently enacted legislation (referred to as Core Law), 3 hours of civil rights updating, and a 3-hour course on Canon of Ethics as adopted by the Ohio Real Estate Commission. When a licensee attains the age of 70 years, the licensee need only complete 9 hours of CE classes every three years to keep an active license. The 9 hours must consist of 3 hours of core law, 3 hours of fair housing/civil rights, and 3 hours of ethics. If a licensee is 70 years of age and older AND is inactive, no CE is required.

√ **Note:** All state exam questions assume *everyone* takes 30 hours of CE!

Timing of Continuing Education

A salesperson's CE is due on or before the licensee's birthday, beginning three years after the licensee's first birthday after the initial date of licensure, and every three years thereafter on or before the licensee's birthday.

Example
_____

If you were licensed as a salesperson on September 10, 2010, and your birthday is February 20th, your continuing education will be due three years after your birthday after initial licensure. So in this case, your first birthday after licensure is February 20, 2011, so your first CE requirement is due February 20, 2014, and every three years thereafter.

A salesperson may contact the Division of Real Estate with any questions as to the educational requirements or the dates they are due.

All licensees are required to submit proof that they have completed their 30 hours of continuing education by their due date. A compliance form, R-109, is available on the Ohio Division of Real Estate's website. This form must be submitted along with proof of the licensee's education.

Continuing Education (CE) Course Requirements

Three (3) classroom hours of CE must be taken in a course dedicated exclusively to instruction in recently enacted municipal, state, and federal civil rights laws, civil rights case law, desegregation issues, and methods of eliminating effects of prior discrimination.

Three (3) classroom hours out of the total required thirty (30) hours of continuing education must be taken in a legal update "core law" course. This is a course devoted exclusively to instruction in recently enacted state and federal legislation affecting the real estate industry, including, but not limited to, relevant state real estate licensing laws and regulations, recent court decisions, and related reports.

In addition, in each three-year period, three (3) classroom hours out of the total required thirty (30) hours of continuing education must be taken in a course devoted to the instruction in the Canons of Ethics as adopted by the Ohio Real Estate Commission.

Twenty-one (21) classroom hours of continuing education electives of choice must be taken that are approved by the Ohio Division of Real Estate.

Licensees may take more than 30 hours of CE, but only up to 10 extra hours can count towards future three-year periods. And no more than 8 hours of CE may be taken per day.

The Ohio Division of Real Estate maintains a list of all courses that have been approved for continuing education and that are currently being offered. All approved CE courses are available in a searchable format at the Division's website or you may request a copy of this list by contacting the Division.

Failure to Meet Continuing Education Requirements

If the continuing education requirements are not fulfilled by the due date, the license is automatically suspended and must be returned to the Division of Real Estate.

If a license is suspended, the licensee has twelve months from the date of the suspension in which to take the education and reactivate the license. In order to reactivate a license, the licensee must submit proof of completing the 30 classroom hours of continuing education, submit the compliance form, a reactivation application, and the required fee.

If the required 30 hours are not completed within the grace period, the license is **revoked** and the party must reapply and be tested again in order to become re-licensed.

Exemptions to Continuing Education Requirements

1. Foreign real estate dealers and salespersons aren't required to take continuing education.

2. Licensees who attain 70 years of age need only complete 9 hours of CE classes during the CE cycle in which they turn 70 and every three years thereafter to keep an active license. The 9 hours must consist of 3 hours of core law, 3 hours of fair housing/civil rights and 3 hours of ethics.

3. If a licensee enters the armed forces, the licensee may place their license on deposit until the next renewal date after honorable discharge from the armed services.

There are no other exemptions. If a license is returned to the Division by a broker or by the licensee, the license status is **inactive**. A license may remain inactive indefinitely, as long as it is renewed annually and continuing education requirements are met. Reactivation of a license will not be permitted unless proof of completion of the required continuing education has been received, along with the appropriate applications and fees.

Continuing Education Requirements
All licensees must take:
1. 30 hours every 3 years*
2. 3 hours: Civil Rights
3. 3 hours: Core Law
4. 3 hours: Canons of Ethics
5. If not completed, licensed is suspended
6. 1-year grace period to complete or licensed revoked
For those who reach the age of 70, they must only complete 9 hours every three years.

License Renewal

Each license issued is valid without further recommendation or examination until revoked or suspended. However, all licenses must be renewed every three (3) years *on or before the licensee's birthday in the calendar year during which the licensee's continuing education is due.* The Division of Real Estate sends each licensee, via regular mail, an **Renewal Notice prior to the licensee's birthday**. The licensee is responsible for renewing on or before the licensee's birthday, regardless of whether or not a renewal notice is received. The cost of renewal for sales licenses is $135.00 each three years, with a 50% penalty if filed after the filing deadline. Broker license renewal fee is $180.00 each three years.

If a broker is **not** going to keep a salesperson, he must notify the salesperson of that decision within 3 days of the day of return of the license to the Division.

The license of any real estate broker or salesperson who fails to renew a license by failing to file an application of renewal prior to the filing deadline shall be inactivated.

Inactivation. A broker who chooses to terminate association with a salesperson must send the salesperson's license back to the Division of Real Estate and notify the salesperson within three days, in writing via certified mail, that the license has been sent to the Division of Real Estate for inactivation.

If a salesperson is not renewed by his or her broker, the salesperson's license is no longer valid. However, if the salesperson associates with a new broker, the salesperson is permitted to request license reactivation within a twelve month period. After twelve months, if a salesperson wants a new license, he or she must retake the salesperson exam.

The death of a broker or the suspension or revocation of the broker's license also inactivates all of the broker's salespersons' licenses, pending a change of broker or issuance of a new license.

Transfer

If a broker decides not to renew a salesperson's license, or if the salesperson simply wants to change jobs, or the broker's license has been suspended or revoked, the salesperson may become associated with a new broker. If a salesperson wishes to become associated with a different broker, it is necessary to transfer the salesperson's license to the new broker. In order to do so, the current broker must submit the salesperson's license to the Division of Real Estate. The Superintendent may transfer the license of a salesperson to a new broker without the return of salesperson's license, provided the salesperson certifies on the transfer application that he/she provided notice to the former broker of the intent to transfer to a new broker and that the notification was in writing. The salesperson must file a sales transfer application form along with a $20.00 fee. Broker license transfer fee is $25.00. Once these are received, a new salesperson license will be issued and sent to the new broker.

Licenses can be transferred at any time during the year.

Department of Commerce

Division of Real Estate
& Professional Licensing

John R. Kasich, Governor   77 South High Street, 20th Floor
David Goodman, Director   Columbus, Ohio 43215-6133 U.S.A.

Please visit our website at
www.com.ohio.gov/real

614 | 466-4100
Fax 614 | 644-0584
TTY/TDD: 800 | 750-0750

RENEWAL APPLICATION WITH EDUCATION COMPLIANCE FORM

BROKER RENEWAL FEE: $180
SALESPERSON RENEWAL FEE: $135

Online Renewal:

➢ Go to www.com.ohio.gov/real

➢ Click *eLicense Center* under the Online Services heading.

➢ Choose the *Renew Your Real Estate License* link.

➢ Click the Login button to sign-on to our secure site and login using your User ID and password.

➢ Answer the Ethical Conduct and Legal History questions.

➢ Pay your renewal fee online using a Visa or MasterCard. *Credit card information may not be taken over the telephone.*

➢ Print out the receipt page for your records.

➢ **Send a Continuing Education Compliance Form and continuing education certificates to the address below by your due date.**

➢ **Mail to:** Ohio Division of Real Estate & Professional Licensing

77 S. High Street, 20th floor

Columbus, Ohio 43215-6133

Note: If Online Renewal is unavailable, it is the licensee's obligation to make certain the renewal is timely filed.

Mail-In Renewal:

➢ Complete the Renewal Application and the Continuing Education Compliance form and attach the proof of completion certificates, if applicable.

➢ Answer the Ethical Conduct and Legal History questions.

➢ Sign the Renewal Application (page 1) and the Continuing Education Compliance form (page 3).

➢ Return the forms and education certificates, **along with the renewal fee,** to the Division. Make the check or money order payable to Ohio Division of Real Estate. Cash will not be accepted.

➢ **Mail to:** Ohio Division of Real Estate & Professional Licensing

77 S. High Street, 20th floor

Columbus, Ohio 43215-6133

RENEWAL REMINDERS:

- The Renewal Application and Education Compliance Form will not be accepted earlier than 60 days before your due date.
- If this is your first birthday since becoming licensed, your renewal is due, but not your 30 hours of continuing education.

I am renewing my (check one)   ☐ BROKER LICENSE ($180)   FILE NUMBER: _____

☐ SALESPERSON LICENSE ($135)   FILE NUMBER: _____

FIRST NAME	MIDDLE NAME	LAST NAME	DATE OF BIRTH (mm/dd/yyyy)
HOME ADDRESS ☐ Check if new.			HOME PHONE ( )
CITY		STATE	ZIP CODE + 4
E-MAIL ADDRESS			

ETHICAL CONDUCT AND LEGAL HISTORY

▪ PLEASE **ATTACH A COMPLETE EXPLANATION** FOR ANY QUESTIONS ANSWERED "**YES.**"

▪ QUESTIONS CONCERNING PROFESSIONAL LICENSES APPLY TO **ALL PROFESSIONAL LICENSES** REGARDLESS OF PROFESSION.

SINCE your most recent filing of an application for Ohio real estate licensure, renewal or transfer/reactivation application, have you:

☐YES ☐NO   been disciplined in any manner by any public entity or professional or trade association for any violation of any professional licensing law, regulation or ethical rule?

☐YES ☐NO   been refused or denied any professional license or registration by any public entity?

☐YES ☐NO   had any professional license revoked, suspended or limited in any way for any reason?

☐YES ☐NO   been notified by any public entity or professional or trade association that you were under investigation for any violation of any professional licensing law, regulation or ethical rule?

☐YES ☐NO   been the subject of any unsatisfied judgments?

☐YES ☐NO   been convicted of, plead guilty to or been granted intervention in lieu of conviction for any unlawful conduct excluding minor traffic violations? LIST:

THE APPLICANT MUST COMPLETE THE FOLLOWING CERTIFICATION

I certify that all of the statements on this application and all of the attached materials are complete and accurate. I understand that any false statement on this form or any attached materials may subject me to criminal prosecution and the loss of my Ohio real estate license.

_____   _____
SIGNATURE OF APPLICANT   DATE

COM 3681 (Rev. 02/2011)   *"An Equal Opportunity Employer and Service Provider"*   Page 1 of 3

REAL ESTATE CONTINUING EDUCATION COMPLIANCE FORM

Proof of Continuing Education Compliance may not be submitted earlier than 60 days before the due date.

Each licensee shall submit proof to the superintendent that the licensee has satisfactorily completed thirty (30) hours of continuing education, including the three required courses in **Civil Rights, Core Law,** and **Canons of Ethics.**

Each licensee who is seventy (70) years of age or older within a continuing education reporting period shall submit proof that the licensee has completed a total of nine (9) hours of continuing education, including the three required courses in **Civil Rights, Core Law,** and **Canons of Ethics.** A licensee who is seventy (70) years of age or older during the reporting period whose license is in Inactive status is exempt from the continuing education requirements specified in this section.

- Sign the certification below and enter the date.
- Enter your name and File Number (license number).
- List each course completed and enclose a copy of the attendance certificate to verify state certification and date of offering.
- **Carry–Over Hours:**
  - List carry-over hours from your last reporting period, which you are using for credit this period, under ELECTIVES.
  - List hours that you took this reporting period that you wish to carry-over to the next reporting period (up to 10 hours) in the CARRY-OVER section on page 3.

THE APPLICANT MUST COMPLETE THE FOLLOWING CERTIFICATION

I certify that all of the statements on this Continuing Education Compliance Form and all of the attached materials are complete and accurate. I understand that any false statement on this compliance form or any of the attached materials may subject me to criminal prosecution and the loss of my Ohio real estate license. I attest that I did, in fact, attend the courses listed for at least 90 percent of the time indicated.

_____   _____
SIGNATURE OF APPLICANT   DATE

LICENSEE NAME	LICENSEE FILE NUMBER	
CIVIL RIGHTS COURSE (MINIMUM 3 HOURS)		
COURSE PROVIDER	STATE CERTIFICATION (APPROVAL) NUMBER	HOURS
COURSE TITLE	DATE(S) OF ATTENDANCE	
CORE LAW COURSE (MINIMUM 3 HOURS)		
COURSE PROVIDER	STATE CERTIFICATION (APPROVAL) NUMBER	HOURS
COURSE TITLE	DATE(S) OF ATTENDANCE	
CANONS OF ETHICS COURSE (MINIMUM 3 HOURS)		
COURSE PROVIDER	STATE CERTIFICATION (APPROVAL) NUMBER	HOURS
COURSE TITLE	DATE(S) OF ATTENDANCE	
ELECTIVES		
COURSE PROVIDER	STATE CERTIFICATION (APPROVAL) NUMBER	HOURS
COURSE TITLE	DATE(S) OF ATTENDANCE	
COURSE PROVIDER	STATE CERTIFICATION (APPROVAL) NUMBER	HOURS
COURSE TITLE	DATE(S) OF ATTENDANCE	
COURSE PROVIDER	STATE CERTIFICATION (APPROVAL) NUMBER	HOURS
COURSE TITLE	DATE(S) OF ATTENDANCE	
COURSE PROVIDER	STATE CERTIFICATION (APPROVAL) NUMBER	HOURS
COURSE TITLE	DATE(S) OF ATTENDANCE	
COURSE PROVIDER	STATE CERTIFICATION (APPROVAL) NUMBER	HOURS
COURSE TITLE	DATE(S) OF ATTENDANCE	
COURSE PROVIDER	STATE CERTIFICATION (APPROVAL) NUMBER	HOURS
COURSE TITLE	DATE(S) OF ATTENDANCE	

ADDITIONAL SPACE IS PROVIDED ON PAGE 3   Page 2 of 3

COURSE PROVIDER	STATE CERTIFICATION (APPROVAL) NUMBER	HOURS
COURSE TITLE	DATE(S) OF ATTENDANCE	
COURSE PROVIDER	STATE CERTIFICATION (APPROVAL) NUMBER	HOURS
COURSE TITLE	DATE(S) OF ATTENDANCE	
COURSE PROVIDER	STATE CERTIFICATION (APPROVAL) NUMBER	HOURS
COURSE TITLE	DATE(S) OF ATTENDANCE	
COURSE PROVIDER	STATE CERTIFICATION (APPROVAL) NUMBER	HOURS
COURSE TITLE	DATE(S) OF ATTENDANCE	
COURSE PROVIDER	STATE CERTIFICATION (APPROVAL) NUMBER	HOURS
COURSE TITLE	DATE(S) OF ATTENDANCE	

TOTAL HOURS FROM PAGES 2 & 3 (MUST = 30)
(Total hours for licensees over 70 years of age must = 9)

LIST UP TO TEN HOURS OF CARRY-OVER EDUCATION BELOW. If you did not use all of the hours of the last class listed above to reach the 30 total hours, list that class first here with any of the carry over hours.

COURSE PROVIDER	STATE CERTIFICATION (APPROVAL) NUMBER	HOURS
COURSE TITLE	DATE(S) OF ATTENDANCE	
COURSE PROVIDER	STATE CERTIFICATION (APPROVAL) NUMBER	HOURS
COURSE TITLE	DATE(S) OF ATTENDANCE	
COURSE PROVIDER	STATE CERTIFICATION (APPROVAL) NUMBER	HOURS
COURSE TITLE	DATE(S) OF ATTENDANCE	
COURSE PROVIDER	STATE CERTIFICATION (APPROVAL) NUMBER	HOURS
COURSE TITLE	DATE(S) OF ATTENDANCE	
COURSE PROVIDER	STATE CERTIFICATION (APPROVAL) NUMBER	HOURS
COURSE TITLE	DATE(S) OF ATTENDANCE	
COURSE PROVIDER	STATE CERTIFICATION (APPROVAL) NUMBER	HOURS
COURSE TITLE	DATE(S) OF ATTENDANCE	
COURSE PROVIDER	STATE CERTIFICATION (APPROVAL) NUMBER	HOURS
COURSE TITLE	DATE(S) OF ATTENDANCE	
	TOTAL CARRY OVER HOURS	

Location and Display of License

Broker. Every broker is required by law to maintain a definite place of business and to construct a sign at such place which states that the broker is a real estate broker. **The broker must be identified in the sign at the place of business, as well as in any advertising**.

The license of a broker must be prominently displayed in the office or place of business of the broker next to the Equal Housing and Opportunity poster which is required by federal and Ohio law. The license of a salesperson must be kept on file by the broker with whom the salesperson is associated. A salesperson's license must be kept in such a way that it can, on request, be made immediately available for public inspection at the office or place of business of the principal broker (not the branch offices—branch license should be prominently displayed next to the Equal Opportunity Housing (EOH poster).

The license of a salesperson associated with a broker must remain in the possession of the broker until the license is inactivated, or transferred to another broker, or the association ends. **Immediately upon** the termination of the association of a real estate salesperson with the broker (such as when the salesperson quits or is fired), the broker must return the salesperson's license to the Superintendent of Real Estate for inactivation.

Deposit of License of a Salesperson in the Armed Forces

If a broker or salesperson enters the armed forces, the license may also be placed on deposit with the approval of the Commission until the next renewal date after honorable discharge. If the licensee is unable to complete the continuing education requirements because of duties in the armed services, the licensee will have until twelve months after such discharge from the service to complete the continuing education requirements.

Partnership or Corporation

All of the members or officers authorized to perform the functions of a real estate broker as the agents of a partnership, association, limited liability partnership, limited liability company, or corporation which is a licensed real estate broker must be licensed individually as real estate brokers. However, no real estate broker who is a member of a partnership, association, limited liability partnership, limited liability company, or corporation which is a licensed real estate broker may perform any acts as a real estate broker other than as the agent of the partnership, association, limited liability partnership, limited liability company, or corporation. An individual broker working with a partnership, association, limited liability partnership, limited liability company, or corporation as a principal in the partnership, association, limited liability partnership, limited liability company, or corporation may not have any real estate salesperson associated with him or her individually.

Fees	
Fees are set by statute and increase from time to time. The Ohio Revised Code states the current fee schedule.	
Broker's examination application fee paid to the division	$100 *
Salesperson's examination application fee paid to the division	$60 *
Broker certificate of continuation (renewal)	$180
Salesperson certificate of continuation (renewal)	$135
Salesperson license transfer	$25
Broker license transfer (into or out of partnership or corporation)	$25
Branch office license	$15
Foreign real estate dealer's license and each annual renewal salesperson	$30 **
Foreign real estate salesperson's license and each annual renewal	$50
Replacement of lost or damaged license (broker or sales)	$20
Addition of DBA ("Doing Business As" name) to license	$20
Name change for an individual, corporation, or partnership	$20
Reservation of name	$10
Certification of Licensure	$20

Plus testing fee payable directly to examination service

**Per salesperson, but no less than $150*

Use of Fees

All fees collected are paid to the Treasurer of State. In Ohio, fees from both brokers and salespersons are divided among three funds: The Education and Research Fund, the Real Estate Recovery Fund, and the Division of Real Estate Operating Fund.

Real Estate Education and Research Fund

The Real Estate Education and Research Fund was created:

1. To advance the cause of education and research in real estate at any institution of higher education in the state.

2. To make loans (not exceeding $2,000) to applicants for salesperson licenses to defray the costs of satisfying the pre-license educational requirements. A loan from real estate education and research fund must be repaid within one year.

Money for the fund is provided from fees paid by licensees. Out of every fee that is collected, such as for license applications, transfers, and license renewals, $1.00 of the fee is put into the Real Estate Education and Research Fund.

Loans. An individual may apply for a loan to defray the costs of satisfying the educational requirements. The application must be made in writing on a form provided by the Superintendent. The application must include:

1. A statement that the loan is necessary for the completion of courses required for licensing

2. The title or titles of the educational courses for which the loan is sought

3. The full name and address of the accredited institution(s) at which the course(s) will be taken

4. The cost of tuition and required texts for the course(s)

5. The name of the broker sponsoring the license and loan applicant

The sponsoring broker serves as guarantor of the loan and is liable to the Education and Research Fund for any amount outstanding on default by the applicant. If after licensing, the loan recipient transfers to a different broker, the new broker must assume in writing the guaranty responsibility.

Disbursements from the Education and Research Fund for personal education loans are made directly to the applicant. The funds must be used solely for the payment of expenses for tuition and books for the courses reported on the individual's loan application form.

Repayment. Repayment of loan funds is made on the following terms:

Loans and Repayment
1. Pre-licensing only
2. $2,000 maximum
3. Paid back interest free
4. 1/3 due in 6 months after license is issued
5. 1/3 due in 9 months after license is issued
6. Balance due in 12 months after license is issued
7. In any event, no longer than 3 years from disbursement of loan
8. Broker must co-sign as a guarantor for any loan
9. Family size and income determine the amount of the loan

If the applicant has not been licensed as a real estate salesperson within one year of the date of disbursement from the fund, the full amount shall immediately become due, unless that individual demonstrates that he or she is scheduled to take the salesperson license examination. In no event shall any individual's indebtedness to the fund continue beyond three years from the date of disbursement. Any amount outstanding at that time shall immediately become due.

Example

Bart received a loan from the fund in September 1998, but never got around to taking the exam. He decided not to go into real estate after all. In September, 1999, the full amount of the loan is due.

Someone who has previously failed to satisfactorily complete a course for which costs were defrayed by a loan from the fund may not apply again for further loan funds.

No one will be approved for admission to the broker license examination who has not repaid in full any obligation incurred to the Education and Research Fund.

Real Estate Recovery Fund

The Real Estate Recovery Fund is created in the State Treasury and is administered by the Superintendent of Real Estate. The minimum balance for this fund is $500,000.00. The Commission imposes a special assessment requiring that up to $10 of each license renewal or transfer fee go into this account when the fund falls below $500,000.00. If the fund is between $500,000.00 and $2 million, then up to $5 may be taken. If the fund is above $2 million, then no amounts will be taken.

Purpose. Money from this fund is used to satisfy unpaid claims against a broker or salesperson who has been judged to have violated the real estate law in a way that caused financial harm to someone.

Procedure. Claims are made in the court of common pleas by parties who have a final court judgment for damages against a broker or salesperson. The party making the claim files an application for payment, along with evidence that he or she has diligently pursued all other avenues to receive payment but has been unsuccessful.

The Superintendent **cannot** make payment out of the fund **without a court order**. The court will order the Superintendent to make payment out of the Real Estate Recovery Fund when the person seeking the order has shown all of the following:

1. Judgment has been obtained.

2. All appeals from the judgment have been exhausted, and notice has been given to the Superintendent as required.

3. The applicant is not the spouse or the personal representative of the spouse of the judgment debtor (the licensee).

4. The applicant has diligently pursued all remedies against all judgment debtors and all other persons liable in the transaction for which recovery is sought.

5. The application is made not more than one year after termination of all proceedings, including appeals, in connection with the judgment.

Limits. The law limits the amount of claims to be paid from the fund against any one broker or salesperson to **$40,000**. Note that this limit is per licensee, not per violation. If the $40,000 is insufficient to pay all of the parties who have filed claims against any one licensee, then the $40,000 is distributed among them in the same ratio that their respective claims bear to the total amount of valid claims (or in such other manner as the court finds equitable).

Example

1. A broker and two of his salespeople were involved in a real estate fraud scheme. They defrauded Adams for over $200,000. Adams received a court judgment against them, but was unable to recover any of the money. Adams filed an application for payment from the Real Estate Recovery Fund. Adams received $120,000 (a maximum of $40,000 for each broker and salesperson involved).

2. A broker defrauded several different clients. Atkins lost $20,000, Baker lost $30,000, Carlton lost $45,000, and Davis lost $5,000. They all received court judgments against the broker but were unable to recover any of the money. They filed applications for payment from the Real Estate Recovery Fund. The maximum amount that could be paid was $40,000. Each received a percentage according to their percentage of the total amount of valid claims. Atkins received 20% or $8,000; Baker received 30% or $12,000; Carlton received 45% or $18,000; and Davis received 5% or $2,000.

All claims to the Recovery Fund must be made within one year after the final court judgment. Payment from the Recovery Fund is only for amounts that represent the actual and direct loss suffered by the applicant. Punitive damages and interest are not recoverable from the Fund. At the discretion of the Superintendent of Real Estate, attorney fees and court costs may be recovered from the Fund.

Payment out of the Fund is also limited to damages arising out of real estate services. If the judgment had nothing to do with a licensee's professional acts, only personal ones, the Recovery Fund could not be used. For example, if a salesperson was involved in a boating accident and was found liable for damages to an injured party, the injured party could not apply to the Real Estate Recovery Fund, because the judgment had nothing to do with the salesperson's real estate activity.

Affect on Salesperson or Broker. If the Superintendent pays from the Fund any amount in settlement of a claim against a licensed broker or salesperson, the license of the broker or salesperson is **automatically suspended on the date of payment from the Fund**. No broker or salesperson will be reactivated until the licensee has repaid in full, plus interest, the amount paid from the Fund on the licensee's account. Filing bankruptcy does not relieve the licensee of the suspension and requirement of repayment before reactivation.

Repaying the Fund does not automatically reactivate the license. If other independent grounds exist for the suspension of the license, it can remain suspended.

Real Estate Recovery Fund

1. Superintendent administers
2. Insolvent licensee
3. Needs final judgment
4. Appeals are complete
5. Debtor is not their spouse
6. Apply less than 1 year from appeal being completed
7. Maximum liability of Fund is $40,000 per licensee
8. Condition of license reactivation is repayment plus interest
9. $500,000.00 to $2 million

Complaint Procedures

The Complaint Process is a method where *any person* can ask the Division of Real Estate to investigate alleged violations of Ohio real estate license law. Complaints may be filed/initiated by any person.

The procedure is for consumers, as well as licensees, who have evidence that Ohio real estate law has been violated. Disputes between licensees that may or may not pertain to license law can be heard by arbitration committees of the local Board of REALTORS ®. If a licensee is not a member of the REALTOR® Board, then a remedy may be sought through the state courts.

Disciplinary Action

Upon receiving a verified written complaint, the Superintendent must investigate the actions of a licensee if the Superintendent determines that the complaint is within the Division's jurisdiction. Within five business days after a person files a signed, written complaint against a licensee, the Superintendent acknowledges receipt of the complaint and sends a notice to the licensee describing the particulars of the complaint, by certified mail.

The acknowledgment to the complainant and the notice to the licensee state that a mediation meeting will be held with the complainant, the licensee, and an investigator, if the complainant and the licensee both file a request for such a meeting within ten business days on a form provided by the Superintendent.

Mediation Meeting. If both parties file the form requesting the mediation meeting, the Superintendent schedules a mediation meeting with the parties involved and a Division mediator. The Superintendent notifies the complainant and licensee of the date of the meeting, which is within twenty business days after the request for the meeting. Any party may request an extension of up to fifteen business days for good cause. If the parties reach an agreement at the mediation meeting, the mediator informs the Superintendent and the parties to the complaint, and the complaint file is closed. However, if a pattern of repeat allegations is evident, the Superintendent may refuse mediation and open an investigation.

The Superintendent may also commence an investigation upon his or her own initiative. A broker's or salesperson's license may be suspended or revoked if the licensee is found guilty of violating the Ohio Real Estate Law.

Statute Of Limitations. Since violations are subject to the statute of limitations, the Superintendent may only commence an investigation against a licensee if the complaint is filed within three years from the date of the alleged violation. If it has been more than three years since the alleged violation occurred, the statutory period has passed, an investigation is barred, and no disciplinary action can be taken against the licensee.

Procedure. If the parties do not agree to a mediation meeting, or hold a meeting but are unable to reach a settlement, or if there is evidence of a serious license violation and the Superintendent chooses to proceed with the case, the Superintendent notifies the parties and orders an investigation.

Within sixty business days after receipt of the complaint, or if a mediation meeting was held, within sixty days of the meeting, the investigator files a written report with the Superintendent. All information that is obtained by investigators and auditors and all reports and documents must be held in confidence by the Superintendent, the investigators and auditors, and other personnel of the department.

Within ten business days after the submission of the investigator's report, the Superintendent reviews the report and determines if there exists reasonable and substantial evidence of a violation of the law. If there is such evidence, the Superintendent notifies the parties and schedules a formal hearing within seven to fifteen days thereafter. Any party may request an extension of up to thirty days for good cause.

If the Superintendent decides that there is not sufficient evidence to justify a formal hearing, the Superintendent notifies the complainant and the licensee. The complainant has the right to ask the Commission to review the Superintendent's decision. If such a request is filed within 15 days, the Commission reviews the decision at its next regularly scheduled meeting. At the request of either party, the Commission will hear testimony from either party at their meeting.

If the Commission agrees with the Superintendent's decision, the complainant and licensee are so notified within five business days. If the Commission does not agree and reverses the Superintendent's decision, the parties are notified that a formal hearing will be held.

The Formal Hearing. The Superintendent appoints hearing examiners to preside over the formal hearings. In appointing a hearing examiner, the Superintendent gives preference to attorneys with experience and expertise in real estate.

After notice of a hearing has been forwarded to the licensee by certified mail, one continuance or postponement may be granted to the licensee. The request for continuance must be made in writing and must be received by the Superintendent more than 48 hours before the scheduled time of the hearing. Additional continuances or postponements of the hearing may be granted at the discretion of the Superintendent for good cause shown. The Division may also continue any hearing upon its own motion.

The licensee may appear at the hearing with or without legal counsel, but it is recommended that any licensee involved in these proceedings consult an attorney from the beginning. Testimony is taken under oath. Either the Commission or Superintendent can compel the attendance of witnesses at hearings and the production of documents in the witnesses' possession. Their powers are the same as county court judges. They can administer oaths, compel witness attendance, or impose punishment on a witness who refuses to testify. They may also file an application with any Ohio Common Pleas Court for assistance. The court may then subpoena the witness or order the production of documents. If the witness fails to obey the court, the court may order the person arrested and jailed for contempt of court.

Review. Within twenty-five business days after the conclusion of the formal hearing, the hearing examiner files a report of findings of fact and conclusions of law with the Superintendent, the Commission, and the parties. The Commission reviews this report at its next regularly scheduled meeting. The Commission will hear the testimony of any party upon request. Within sixty days of the filing of the hearing examiner's report, the Commission decides whether to impose discipline which may include revocation or suspension of the licensee's real estate license.

The Commission must maintain a transcript of the proceedings and must issue a written opinion to all of the parties, citing its findings and grounds for any action taken. If there is a financial loss involved, the injured party is advised that he or she may apply to the Real Estate Recovery Fund if unable to recover from the liable licensee.

The licensee has the right to appeal the decision in court. If no appeal is filed, the Ohio Real Estate Commission may consider a motion for reconsideration (asking to change its decision) if the motion for reconsideration is filed prior to the expiration of the time to file an appeal under Ohio law (15 days after a final judgment).

Investigative powers and procedures followed by Ohio Division of Real Estate and Ohio Real Estate Commission include:

- All information obtained by investigators from licensees, complainants, or other persons, and all reports, documents, and work products that arise from that information or are prepared by division employees must be held in confidence.

- An investigation may be commenced against a licensee only if the complaint is filed within three years from the date of the alleged violation. After three years, an investigation is barred and no disciplinary action can be taken against the licensee because of the alleged violation.

- An application to the commission to reverse, vacate, or modify an order must be filed within 15 days after the order is mailed to the party.

Additional grounds for disciplinary action against a licensee include:

- The Ohio Real Estate Commission can suspend or revoke a person's license based on a conviction of any type of felony or crime of moral turpitude, regardless of whether it involved real estate activity.

- Like brokers, salespersons are also subject to disciplinary actions for failing to satisfy a judgment that arose out of conduct as a licensee.

Civil Rights Complaints. If the Ohio Civil Rights Commission files a complaint, it is entitled to have its complaint reviewed by the Real Estate Commission directly upon request instead of going through the entire process. The Real Estate Commission then renders a decision within sixty days of receiving the complaint. If a licensee is convicted of a civil rights violation:

1st offense: License suspension

2nd offense: License suspension or revocation

3rd offense: License revocation

Grounds for Suspension, Revocation, or Denial of a License

The basic grounds for suspension, revocation, or denial of a real estate license are found in the Ohio Revised Code, Section 4735.18 and are as follows: **A number of test questions could relate to the following. This is the area most missed on the state exam**.

1. Knowingly making any misrepresentation

2. Making any false promises with intent to influence, persuade, or induce

3. A continued course of misrepresentation or the making of false promises through agents, salespersons, advertising, or otherwise

4. Unauthorized dual agency acting for more than one party in a transaction without the knowledge or consent of all parties

5. Failure within a reasonable time to account for or to remit any money coming into his possession that belongs to others

6. Dishonest or illegal dealing, gross negligence, incompetence, or misconduct, including a conviction of a felony or a crime involving moral turpitude

7. a) A final judgment by a court of a violation of any municipal or federal civil rights law relevant to the protection of purchasers or sellers of real estate, or a final judgment by a court of any unlawful discriminatory practice pertaining to the purchase or sale of real estate prohibited by Chapter 4112. of the Revised Code, provided that such violation arose out of a situation where parties were engaged in bona fide efforts to purchase, sell, or lease real estate, in his practice as a licensed real estate broker or salesperson

b) A second or subsequent violation of any unlawful discriminatory practice, whether or not there has been a final judgment by a court. For a second offense, the Commission shall suspend for a minimum of two months or revoke the license of the broker or salesperson. For any subsequent offense, the Commission shall revoke the license of the broker or salesperson.

8. Procuring a license by fraud, misrepresentation, or deceit.

9. Having willfully disregarded or violated any provision of Chapter 4735 (Chapter 4735 is the real estate broker and salesperson section of the Ohio Revised Code).

10. Having demanded, without reasonable cause, a commission to which the licensee is not entitled.

11. Having paid commissions or fees to, or divided commissions or fees with, anyone not licensed as a real estate broker or salesperson.

12. Having used any trade name or insignia of membership in any real estate organization of which the licensee is not a member.

13. Having accepted, given, or charged any undisclosed commission, rebate, or direct profit on expenditures made for a principal.

14. Having offered anything of value other than the consideration recited in the sales contract as an inducement to a person to enter into a contract for the purchase or sale of real estate or having offered real estate or the improvements thereon as a prize in a lottery or scheme of chance.

15. Having acted in the dual capacity of broker and undisclosed principal in any transaction.

16. Having guaranteed, authorized, or permitted any person to guarantee future profits which may result from the resale of real property or cemetery interment rights.

17. Having placed a sign on any property offering it for sale or rent without the consent of the owner or his authorized agent.

18. Having induced any party to a contract of sale or lease to break such contract for the purpose of substituting in lieu thereof a new contract with another principal.

19. Having negotiated the sale, exchange, or lease of any real property directly with an owner or lessor knowing that such owner or lessor had a written outstanding contract granting exclusive agency in connection with such property to another real estate broker.

20. Having offered real property for sale or for lease without the knowledge and consent of the owner or the owner's authorized agent, or on any terms other than those authorized by the owner or the owner's authorized agent.

21. Having published advertising, whether printed, radio, display, or of any other nature, which was misleading or inaccurate in any material particular, or in any way having misrepresented any properties, terms, values, policies, or services of the business conducted.

22. Having knowingly withheld from or inserted in any statement of account or invoice any statement that made it inaccurate in any material particular.

23. Having published or circulated unjustified or unwarranted threats of legal proceedings which tended to or had the effect of harassing competitors or intimidating their customers.

24. Having failed to keep complete and accurate records of all transactions for a period of three years from the date of the transaction, such records to include copies of listing forms, earnest money receipts, offers to purchase and acceptances thereof, and records of receipts and disbursements of all funds received by him as broker and incident to his transactions as such, and any other instruments or papers related to the performance of any of the acts set forth in the definition of a real estate broker.

25. Failure of a broker or salesperson to furnish all parties involved in a real estate transaction true copies of all listings and other agreements to which they are a party, at the time each party signs the same.

26. Failing to maintain a trust account separate from broker funds. The account must be a *non*-interest-bearing account with a bank in the state of Ohio. The bank and account number must be provided to the Division as part of a broker application, and kept for inspection by the Investigations and Audit Bureau.

27. Failing to maintain a separate and distinct account for the deposit and maintenance of rents, security deposits, and other money received in the course of managing real property. This account *can* be an interest-bearing account with a bank in the state of Ohio, with interest paid to the property owner. The bank and account number must be provided to the Division as part of a broker application, and kept for inspection by the Investigations and Audit Bureau. Brokers not engaged in property management for others are exempt.

28. Having failed to put definite expiration dates in all written agency agreements to which the broker is a party.

29. Having an unsatisfied final judgment in any court of record against the licensee arising out of the licensee's conduct as a licensed broker or salesperson.

30. Failing to render promptly upon demand a full and complete statement of the expenditures by the broker of funds advanced by or on behalf of an owner to the broker for the purpose of advertising or promoting the sale of the owner's real estate.

31. Failure within a reasonable time, after the receipt of the commission by the broker, to render an accounting to and pay a real estate salesperson the salesperson's earned share thereof.

32. Performing any service for another constituting the practice of law, as determined by any court of law.

33. Having been adjudicated incompetent for the purpose of holding the license by a court. A license revoked or suspended under this Division shall be reactivated upon proof to the Commission of the removal of the disability.

34. As a partnership, association, limited liability partnership, limited liability company, or corporation, having authorized or permitted a person to act as its agent in its capacity as a real estate broker, who was not then licensed as a real estate broker under this chapter.

35. Knowingly inserting any materially inaccurate term in a document, including naming a false consideration.

36. Having failed to inform the licensee's client of the existence of an offer or counter offer in a timely manner, unless otherwise instructed by the client, provided that the instruction does not conflict with any state or federal law.

Whenever the Commission suspends or revokes the license of a salesperson for any of these violations, the Commission may also suspend or revoke the license of the broker with whom the salesperson is affiliated, if the Commission finds the **broker had knowledge** of the salesperson's actions.

The revocation or suspension of a broker's license automatically suspends all sales licenses associated with the broker. When this happens, the associated salespeople may, upon proper application, transfer to another broker.

In addition to suspension or revocation of a license, a licensee may also be fined by the Superintendent up to $200 for each violation (up to a maximum total of $2,500) of agency, advertising, or fair housing language law. If any licensee receives three violation citations within a 12-month period, this causes the Superintendent to initiate disciplinary action, which may result in revocation or suspension of the license. If a licensee does not contest a citation or fine from the Superintendent within 30 days, then the licensee must comply with the Superintendent's orders or face automatic license suspension. These fines by the Superintendent are in addition to fines of up to $2,500 which may also be levied by the Commission for each violation of the Ohio Revised Code. There is no limit to the amount of fines that can be levied by the Commission. Furthermore, a licensee may also be subject to a public reprimand and be ordered to take additional continuing education classes as a condition for reactivation of the license.

Process of Disclosing Inducements

The Division of Real Estate receives many letters and phone calls from licensees asking whether they can legally offer a variety of free items or services to sellers or buyers. Some of these proposed "give-aways" include home warranty plans, carpet cleaning service, tips, gifts certificates, and cash rebates. The concern is whether giving a gift to a buyer or seller will constitute an inducement that is prohibited by license law.

Under Ohio Revised Code Section 4735.18 (A)(14), offering anything of value to a party that is designed to entice or motivate them to enter into a purchase or sale contract is considered to be inducement. Such inducements are *prohibited unless they are disclosed in the purchase contract as part of the consideration.*

Therefore, the license laws do not prohibit a licensee from giving a buyer or seller a free home warranty, weekend get-away, coupons, etc., as long as this fact is disclosed in the purchase contract as part of the consideration to enter into the contract.

It should be noted that the license laws do not prohibit a licensee from paying cash to owners who list property for sale or from paying cash to a customer or client to get them to buy a home, assuming there is proper disclosure. However, the license laws do prohibit giving money or other items of value to an individual who is not a party to the transaction as a referral fee for assisting in procuring the buyer/lessee or for otherwise performing an act that would require a real estate license.

It is also important to note that Section 4735.18(A)(14) does not address inducements to enter into listing contracts. Therefore, such gifts or give-aways can be given to a seller who lists property with a brokerage where receipt of the item is not contingent upon a purchase agreement being entered into. It is recommended, however, that such an agreement be noted on the listing contract to avoid any future disputes or misunderstandings.

In advertising an inducement, brokers must be careful that the terms and value of any item or service being offered are correctly described. Any restrictions or qualifications on participation, or any time limit on the offer should be included in any advertisement in order to avoid a violation of Section 4735.18(A)(21).

Questions concerning the issue of inducements can be directed to the Division's legal section.

Test Your Real Estate Knowledge With Regard To Inducements

The following questions represent typical situations that a licensee may face where inducements can come into play when dealing with the public. Think about these questions, then review the answers on the following page.

1. *Can I advertise the commission rate that I charge?*

2. *Can a broker's listing fee be included in the broker's newspaper advertisement?*

3. *In the area in which I list properties, there is one school district which is very desirable. Is there a fair housing problem if I establish a policy of only advertising the school district for my listings that are in the desirable district, and not advertising the school district on my other listings?*

4. *Can I offer buyers a coupon for a free carpet cleaning or some other type of incentive if they purchase a home through my brokerage?*

5. *Can I give an incentive to buyers to purchase property through my company?*

6. *Are inducements that are given to get people to list or attend an open house regulated under Ohio Laws?*

7. *Is it an inducement if I reduce my commission to get the seller to accept an offer?*

Test Your Real Estate Knowledge with Regard To Inducements Answer Key:

1. Yes. There is nothing in the Code of Ethics, license law, or antitrust laws that prohibits such advertising.

2. Yes.

3. There is a potential steering issue. Steering is the channeling of buyers or tenants to a particular area on the basis of race, color, religion, national origin, or other protected class. This practice is prohibited by the Fair Housing Laws. If you want to advertise the desirable school district, the cautious approach would be to advertise the school district on all your listings. It is best to advertise the school district in all your listings or in none of them.

4. Inducements such as these can be offered if the item being given is recited in the purchase contract as part of the consideration. Be careful when advertising such inducements to make sure that any restrictions or qualifications on participation are clearly stated.

5. Yes. However, this would be considered an inducement under Ohio License Law. As such, it would have to be recited in the purchase contract as part of the consideration.

6. No. Although these "give-aways" may be inducements, they are not prohibited and do not have to be disclosed in the purchase contract. This is because the license law only covers inducements that are given to a buyer or seller to induce them to enter into a purchase contract. It does not cover inducements that are given to entice someone to attend an open house or to list the property. Thus, the items that are given for this purpose are not illegal and are not required to be recited in the purchase contract.

7. If you reduce your commission *prior to* acceptance of an offer, then it is a negotiation of the price of the service. If, *after* acceptance of an offer, you reduce your commission to keep the deal together, then it would be an inducement.

Salesperson's Relationship to Broker Outlined

by: Division of Real Estate Newsletter

The Division of Real Estate has received an increased number of questions and concerns raised by both brokers and salespersons under the real estate license laws.

In prior editions of the Division of Real Estate Newsletter, the importance of having written employment agreements between brokers and salespersons has been discussed. Having a written employment agreement can aid in reducing the risk of misunderstandings by parties regarding their rights and obligations during their association, as well as on termination of their association.

The most common form of real estate employment agreement the Division has observed is usually entitled "Independent Contractor Agreement." However, this type of agreement, although titled as such, does not automatically mean the salesperson is considered a true independent contractor.

In a traditional independent contractor relationship, the independent contractor is a person who contracts with another to perform a certain act according to his own methods and is not subject to the principal's control, other than as to the final result of the work.

However, based on Ohio real estate license laws, a salesperson may not work independently of his licensed broker. Ohio courts have addressed the issue of a salesperson's relationship with a broker and have held that a licensed real estate salesperson has no independent status since the salesperson can only function through the broker with whom he is associated [*Fulton v. Aszman*, 4 Ohio App. 3d 64 (1982)]. Another Ohio court has further held that while a salesperson can be associated with a broker as an independent contractor, the salesperson would not be working independently of the broker (*Burton Minnick Realty, Inc. v. Leffel*, 1990 Ohio App. Lexis 4345).

For example, a real estate salesperson has no right to independently enter into listing agreements with owners or agreements to represent buyers. Further, a salesperson has no right to independently conclude a sale, advertise on his own, directly receive a commission, or maintain an action for a commission from a buyer or seller in a transaction. Rather, these acts must be performed in the name of and through the broker with whom the salesperson is licensed. Likewise, a salesperson cannot provide his sales services to more than one broker at a time.

Accordingly, whether a salesperson's association with a broker is considered to be that of an independent contractor or an employee, for purposes of the real estate license laws, the activities of a licensed salesperson must be approved by and are always under the authority of a broker. A salesperson may engage in the real estate business only on behalf of, and through the licensed broker, with whom he is associated.

It is also important for a broker and salesperson to understand that an agency relationship exists between the salesperson and his associated broker, even though for taxes and other purposes, the salesperson may be considered an independent contractor.

For example, a seller may list his property for sale with a broker under a written listing agreement. Even if the listing is obtained by a salesperson on behalf of the broker, the listing must be taken in the broker's name. The broker, in effect, owns the listing. The broker is then required to act in the best interests of the seller in fulfilling the terms of the listing agreement.

Likewise, agreements by a brokerage to represent a buyer must be obtained in the name of and through the brokerage. Accordingly, when a brokerage enters into an agreement to represent a buyer, all agents associated with the brokerage, directly or indirectly, represent the buyer. For this reason, in transactions where the brokerage has a listing on a particular property, an agent (salesperson) of the listing brokerage cannot agree to solely represent the buyer in the purchase of such property. In this situation, in order for the buyer to also be represented by the brokerage, a *dual agency* relationship is created, which would necessitate the knowledge and consent of all parties to the transaction and the signing of the **written** Agency Disclosure Statement form. Because the process of dual agency is complicated and difficult to practice without breaching a duty to one or both of the parties, *it is recommended that dual agency agreements be obtained by special agreement rather than by a boiler-plate form, and that the broker be consulted when dual agency consent is being sought.*

Role of Non-Licensed Individuals (Personal Assistants) Clarified

Source: Division of Real Estate Newsletter

The Division of Real Estate was asked to clarify the types of activities a non-licensed individual may perform in assisting a real estate licensee. As a basic premise, a real estate license is required for an individual to lawfully engage in conduct set forth in Section 4735.01 of the Ohio Revised Code. Whether an individual is engaged in conduct requiring a real estate license is determined by reviewing the individual's specific conduct. However, there are some guidelines to follow:

Non-Licensee May Perform

A non-licensed individual may perform duties that are secretarial in nature, such as scheduling appointments or calling the owner of properties listed by the brokerage to schedule showings, closings, or inspections. These conversations should be limited to setting an appointment and should not focus on making representations about the services offered by the brokerage.

Although the mere setting of an appointment with an owner is not conduct requiring a real estate license, extreme care must be exercised when a licensed agent authorizes a non-licensed individual to call an owner to set an appointment. A licensee who permits or authorizes a non-licensed individual to perform acts that require a license may be subject to disciplinary action.

Another duty a non-licensed individual can perform is to deliver documents such as offers and counteroffers. However, he cannot answer questions concerning the documents or make any interpretations of those documents.

Non-Licensee May Not Perform

One of the most common questions related to this section is whether a non-licensed individual may prospect or call "for sale by owners" (FSBO) or owners of expired listings to determine their interest in listing or re-listing their property.

While setting an appointment for a licensee would not require a real estate license, asking an owner questions as to their housing needs in order to determine their interest in listing their property may result in the individual needing a license. For example, a non-licensed person calling an owner could have the following dialogue: "My name is John Smith. I'm calling on behalf of Mary Jones of ABC Real Estate to see if an appointment could be set for Mary Jones to discuss the services offered by ABC Real Estate with you." If the response is in the affirmative, an appointment could be set. However, any further inquiries by the non-licensed individual should be avoided.

Based on these parameters, a real estate license would be required to gather information on an owner's house or a home they may be looking for, to provide information to the owner on properties listed, or to request the names of others interested in buying or selling a property.

Ethical Standards

To enhance the professionalism of the real estate industry and to protect the public, the Real Estate Commission has adopted further standards of ethics and professional conduct. All Ohio licensees are bound by the Ohio Canons of Ethics. A licensee found guilty of violating the Canons of Ethics may be charged with misconduct that could result in license suspension or revocation. The law now provides that all licensees are required to take 3 hours of Continuing Education on the Ohio Canons of Ethics.

Canons of Ethics for the Real Estate Industry

Section 1: General Duties to the Public and Industry

Article 1. Licensing as a real estate broker or salesman indicates to the public at large that the individual so designated has special expertise in real estate matters and is subject to high standards of conduct in the licensee's business and personal affairs. The licensee should endeavor to maintain and establish high standards of professional conduct and integrity in dealings with members of the public as well as with fellow licensees and, further, seek to avoid even the appearance of impropriety in any activities as a licensee.

Article 2. It is the duty of the broker to protect the public against fraud, misrepresentation or unethical practices in real estate transactions. The licensee should endeavor to eliminate in the community, any practices which could be damaging to the public or to the integrity of the real estate profession.

Article 3. The licensee should provide assistance wherever possible to the members and staff of the Real Estate Commission and Division of Real Estate in the enforcement of the licensing statutes and administrative rules and regulations adopted in accordance therewith.

Article 4. The licensee should be knowledgeable of the laws of Ohio pertinent to the real estate and should keep informed of changes in the statutes of Ohio affecting the duties and responsibilities of a licensee. (formerly Article 3.1)

Article 5. A licensee should represent clients competently and should promote the advancement of professional education in the real estate industry through the licensee's conduct. (formerly Article 4)

Article 6. The licensee should be informed as to matters affecting real estate in the community, state, and the nation, so that the licensee may be able to contribute to public thinking on such matters including taxation, legislation, land use, city planning, and other questions affecting property interests. (formerly Article 5.1)

Section II: Specific Duties to Clients and Customers

Article 7. The licensee should disclose all known material facts concerning a property on which the licensee is representing a seller or a purchaser to avoid misrepresentation or concealment of material facts. (formerly Article 5.3)

Article 8. The licensee should recommend that title be examined and legal counsel be obtained. (formerly Article 6)

Article 9. The licensee, for the protection of all parties, should see that financial obligations and commitments regarding real estate transactions are in writing, expressing the exact agreement of the parties; and that copies of all agreements, at the time they are executed, are placed in the hands of all parties involved.

Article 10. A licensee should not enter into an agency relationship with a party whose interests are in conflict with those of the licensee or another client represented by the licensee without fully disclosing the potential conflict and obtaining the informed consent of all parties. (formerly Article 11)

Article 11. A licensee should not accept compensation from more than one party without the full knowledge and consent of all parties to the transaction. (formerly Article 12)

Article 12. When acting as a seller's agent, a licensee should disclose to the seller if the licensee is the actual purchaser, or if the purchaser is another licensee affiliated with the same brokerage as the licensee, a business entity in which the licensee has an interest, or is a member of the licensee's immediate family. (formerly Article 13)

Article 13. When asked to provide an appraisal (formal or informal), price opinion, comparative market analysis or any other task that is intended to determine the value of a property, a licensee shall not render that opinion without the careful analysis and interpretation of all factors affecting the property, and should not mislead their client as to the value of the property. (formerly Article 16)

Article 14. The licensee should not undertake to provide professional services concerning a property or its value where the licensee has a present or contemplated interest unless such interest is specifically disclosed to all affected parties. Nor should the licensee make a formal appraisal when the licensee's employment or fee charged for the appraisal is contingent upon the amount of the appraisal. (formerly Article 16. 1)

Article 15. The licensee should not attempt to provide an appraisal, price opinion, comparative market analysis or any other task that is intended to determine the value of a property, if the subject property is of a type that is outside the field of expertise of the licensee unless, the licensee obtains the assistance of another licensee or appraiser who has expertise in this type of property. (formerly Article 16.2)

Article 16. The licensee should not advertise property without authority, and in any advertisement the price quoted should be that agreed upon with the owners as the offering price. (formerly Article 17)

Section III: Duties to Fellow Licensees

Article 17. A licensee should respect the exclusive agency of another licensee until it has expired or until the client, without solicitation initiates a discussion with the licensee about the terms upon which the licensee might enter into a future agency agreement or one commencing upon the expiration of any existing agreement. (former Article 21)

Article 18. A licensee should not solicit a listing that is currently listed with another broker, unless the listing broker, when asked, refuses to disclose the nature and expiration of the listing. In that event the licensee may contact the owner to secure such information and may discuss terms upon which the licensee might take a future listing, or one commencing upon the expiration of any existing exclusive listing. (formerly Article 21.1)

Article 19. A licensee should not solicit a buyer/tenant who is subject to an exclusive buyer/tenant agreement, unless the broker, when asked, refuses to disclose the nature and expiration date of the exclusive buyer/tenant agreement. In that event the licensee may contact the buyer/tenant to secure such information and may discuss the terms upon which the licensee might enter into a future buyer/tenant agreement or may enter into a buyer/tenant agreement to become effective upon the expiration of any existing exclusive buyer/tenant agreement. (new Article)

The National and Ohio Association of REALTORS®

The National Association of REALTORS® (NAR) is a private association that has also written a code of ethics. All members of the National Association of REALTORS® are also bound by the NAR code. The Ohio Association of REALTORS® is a private trade organization. Members of the Ohio Association of REALTORS® also bind themselves to standards of conduct.

It is important to note the distinction between the Ohio Real Estate Canon of Ethics required to be followed by all real estate licensees and the NAR code of ethics. In addition to CE required to satisfy the 3-hour core ethics training under Ohio license law, member Realtors ® must also satisfy a requirement imposed by NAR specific to that association's code of ethics. State-approved ethics courses do NOT satisfy the NAR requirement.

The National and Ohio Associations of REALTORS® do not have the power to suspend or revoke a real estate license. If the Association discovers a member violating the law, it has the duty to inform the Division of Real Estate, which will investigate.

Discrimination

All brokers and salespersons must comply with all federal and state laws prohibiting discrimination. The Federal Fair Housing poster (obtained from the Division of Real Estate' website) must be displayed in every real estate office. This poster contains the equal housing opportunity logo and sets out the federal law concerning illegal discrimination in housing activities.

The Federal Fair Housing Act, regulated by HUD, states that it is illegal to discriminate in the sale, rental, advertising, financing, or appraisal of housing, or in providing brokerage services, because of race, color, religion, sex, disability, familial status, or national origin (and in Ohio Ancestry and Military Status). When HUD investigates a broker for discriminatory practices, it may consider failure to display this poster as prima facie evidence of discrimination.

Information

One of the duties of the Ohio Real Estate Commission is to publish and distribute booklets on housing and remedies for dissatisfied clients. The Division provides pamphlets stating that the broker and salesperson are licensed by the Division of Real Estate and that a client may get in touch with the Division if she has a complaint or inquiry. These pamphlets also contain information concerning the Fair Housing Act and equal housing logo used by HUD. **Brokers and salespeople must make these pamphlets available to their clients.**

Advertising

It is **required** by law that licensees who sell real estate that they own MUST disclose that the owner is a licensed real estate agent in any ads. If a salesperson is not selling the property through his or her broker, the broker's name need not be included. However, the salesperson's own name and the fact that the owner is a licensed real estate agent must be included on all advertising and documents. Indeed, disclosure that a person possesses a real estate license must occur prior to entering into an agreement with a consumer.

When an ad concerning property sold is run through a broker, the broker's name must always be included in the ad. Sometimes, a salesperson's name may also be included in the ad. However, with regard to property sold through a broker, a salesperson's name can never be alone in the ad — the broker's name must **always** be included. In addition, the salesperson's name cannot be more prominent than the broker's name in the ad.

Where a broker has received the approval of the Superintendent to conduct business under a trade name, the trade name, as it appears on the license, is the identifying name that must be used in all advertising.

Disclosure of Agency Relationship

Every licensee preparing or submitting an offer on behalf of a prospective buyer must disclose to the buyer, in writing, the licensee's fiduciary capacity. See chapter 4, Agency Law.

Notification of Conviction

Any licensee convicted of a felony or a crime involving moral turpitude or of violating any federal, state, or municipal civil rights law pertaining to discrimination in housing, or any court which issues a finding of a discriminatory housing practice, shall notify the Superintendent of such conviction or finding within *fifteen* days of the conviction.

If a licensee fails to notify the Superintendent within the required time, the Superintendent may immediately revoke the license of such licensee. Any court which convicts a licensee of a violation of any municipal civil rights law pertaining to housing discrimination also shall notify the Ohio Civil Rights Commission within *fifteen* days of the conviction.

Trust Accounts

A common source of confusion for some licensees is the proper handling of money. Improper handling of funds is one of the major grounds for license revocation or suspension.

Trust Fund. Trust funds are money or other things of value received by a licensee on behalf of a principal or any other person in the performance of any acts for which a real estate license is required, and not belonging to the broker, but being held for the benefit of others.

Handling of Funds. Any real estate licensee who accepts funds in connection with a real estate transaction must handle the funds according to the terms of the contract. Generally, the contract calls for the funds to be deposited into the broker's trust account upon acceptance of the offer by the seller.

If the trust funds are to be retained by the broker; then the trust funds must be retained in the broker's non-interest-bearing trust account until they are disbursed in accordance with the principal's instructions. Separate records must be maintained of all monies received and dispersed from the trust account.

In receiving money from a prospective purchaser, deposit money received by a sales associate must be turned over to the broker. For example, if a salesperson receives a deposit check from a prospective buyer, the check must be given to the broker to be deposited in the broker's trust fund account or in accordance with the terms of the contract. Salespeople may not have trust accounts. *Remember the contract controls the earnest money.*

Property Management Trust Accounts. All brokerages that manage property for another brokerage shall establish and maintain a separate trust account designated as the property management trust account.

There must be enough funds credited to the owner's account to cover expenses that are paid from the property management trust account. Security deposits must also be deposited into this account unless otherwise agreed upon. These accounts may be interest-bearing.

These brokerages shall provide an accounting to each owner of property managed on at least a quarterly basis.

Trust Fund Bank Account. The major reason for establishing and maintaining a separate non-interest-bearing trust account is to avoid any commingling of funds. Trust money must be kept separate from the broker's own general account money. For example, if a broker received an earnest money deposit check from prospective buyers, and the broker placed this money in a general account, this would be considered an unlawful commingling of funds.

Withdrawals. The trust fund bank account must be in the name of the broker as trustee. Withdrawals from a trust fund account may *not* be made without the signature of the broker as trustee, or without the signature of at least one authorized person.

Although the broker can authorize other people to withdraw trust funds, the broker cannot delegate accountability for the funds. The broker is not relieved from compliance with the laws because of the negligence or irresponsibility of an employee. *Note: A broker cannot refund a deposit without a signed release from all the parties to the contract, or a court order directing disbursal or deposit with court of competent jurisdiction.*

Records. Brokers must keep a record of all trust funds received and all trust account records for three years. All records and funds are subject to inspection by the Division of Real Estate during normal business hours and without notice. Brokers must also keep copies of all listings, deposit receipts, canceled checks, and other documents executed or obtained in his capacity as broker for three years, and these records must be available for inspection or audit. We recommend that salespeople do the same.

Commissions

A commission is compensation paid to a broker for services rendered in connection with the sale or exchange of real property. Commissions are negotiated between principal and broker. Commissions are *not* set by law, nor can they be discussed among brokers—this could be construed as price-fixing and violate the Sherman Antitrust Act.

No licensed real estate broker may pay a commission to any person who is not a licensed real estate broker or salesperson, for the sale of another's real estate. A salesperson may only receive compensation (generally a pre-set share of the commission), from her own employing broker. A broker may receive a commission from anyone, even a broker in another state. Commissions may also be paid to licensed brokers of other states as referral fees.

No real estate salesperson may collect any money in connection with a real estate brokerage transaction, whether as commission, deposit, payment, rental, etc., except in the name of, and with consent of, the licensed real estate broker with whom the salesperson is associated. Commission disputes are not actionable by the Superintendent of real estate.

When there is a dispute between the broker and salesperson over the commission on a sale, it may be resolved by court action or by arbitration. No salesperson may commence or maintain any action for a commission or other compensation in connection with a real estate brokerage transaction against any person, except the licensed real estate broker under whom the salesperson was licensed at the time the cause of action arose.

Fair Housing

There are only a few basic laws that you need to have an understanding of in order to answer exam questions regarding civil rights and discrimination laws correctly. The primary thing to keep in mind is that you must be CONSERVATIVE. Many of these questions are common-sense. For instance:

Example

#1:

Q. An out-of-towner says he wants an all-white neighborhood. How do you reply?

A. The safest answer is "I'm sorry. It is illegal for me to discuss those issues."

#2:

Q. Buyers come in and ask you, "How's the school system?" How do you reply?

A. The safest way to answer is to never give your own opinion. If there are facts or statistics on schools prepared by others, that may be okay—ask your broker.

You must remember the only basis on which to legally discriminate is economic, meaning that income or credit history makes prospective buyers unqualified for a particular purchase.

FEDERAL FAIR HOUSING LAWS

The primary laws to know for the exam are the following:

- Civil Rights Act of 1866
- Federal Fair Housing Act of 1968
- Jones v. Mayer (Supreme Court case decision) 1968
- Ohio Civil Rights Laws

Civil Rights Act of 1866

The Civil Rights Act of 1866 basically stated that all citizens, whites and blacks, have the same rights to inherit, purchase, lease, hold, and convey real and/or personal property. In other words, when it comes to race, you could not discriminate in the sale or rental of housing or with regard to personal property. No exceptions!

Fair Housing Act of 1968

This was the primary legislative act that had the greatest impact on housing and discrimination. The original Fair Housing Act of 1968 stated it was illegal to discriminate in the sale or rental of housing based on race, color, religion, or national origin, with certain exemptions or exceptions.

Sex was added to this act in 1974, as was familial status (families with children under 18), and disability in 1988. As of today, the Federal Fair Housing Act prohibits discrimination based on race, color, religion, sex, national origin, familial status, and disability.

Prohibited discrimination includes:

- refusing to sell, rent, or negotiate with any person
- changing the terms of a transaction for certain people
- discriminatory advertising
- wrongly representing that a house is unavailable
- blockbusting—inducing an owner to sell by representing that minorities will be moving into the neighborhood
- redlining—refusing to make loans or provide insurance to persons in certain areas, without regard to their qualifications
- steering—leading prospective homeowners to or away from certain areas based on race, creed, color, etc.
- denying membership in MLS services, real estate brokers' organization, or other facility related to the sale or rental of dwellings as a means of discrimination

Exemptions

The following were exempted under the Federal Fair Housing Act:

Note: Exemptions A & B are **not** recognized under Ohio Fair Housing Act):

A. Single family homes, if owner-occupied, as long as no more than three such sales took place within a two-year period

B. An owner-occupied dwelling, if four or fewer units

C. Private clubs who let only their members rent or occupy rooms

D. Religious group permitting only members of its religion to rent or occupy its dwelling units, as long as the religion did not restrict its membership on the basis of race or national origin

These exemptions were only legal if no advertising or brokerage services were utilized.

Fair Housing Poster

The Fair Housing poster suggested by HUD is required by the Ohio Division of Real Estate to be displayed in the broker's office.

Americans with Disabilities Act

The Americans with Disabilities Act (ADA) expanded the accommodations that must be made for disabled people as a means of prohibiting discrimination. One focus of the ADA is buildings designed to serve the public. All new construction as of Jan. 26, 1993 and all building renovations must be in compliance.

Jones v. Mayer – 1968

Jones v. Mayer was a landmark Supreme Court decision in that it reenacted the original Civil Rights Act of 1866. It stated that when it came to race in regard to the sale or rental of housing there were **no exceptions or exemptions.**

Ohio Civil Rights Laws

The Ohio Civil Rights law is found in Chapter 4112 of the Ohio Revised Code. This section bars discrimination in housing based on race, color, religion, sex, national origin, ancestry, disability, or military status. Since 1992, Ohio law includes discrimination based on familial status and disability as well.

Civil Rights Commission 4112.02. 4112.02 Unlawful Discriminatory Practice

(The following sections are only those which apply to real estate.)

(H) For any person to:

(1) Refuse to self, transfer, assign, rent, lease, sublease, or finance housing accommodations, refuse to negotiate for the sale or rental of housing accommodations, or otherwise deny or make unavailable housing accommodations because of the race, color, religion, sex, ancestry, disability, national origin, or military status of any prospective owner, occupant, or user of the housing.

(2) Represent to any person that housing is not available for inspection, sale, or rental, when in fact it is available, because of the race, color, religion, sex, ancestry, disability, national origin, or military status of any prospective owner, occupant, or user of the housing.

(3) Refuse to lend money, whether or not secured by mortgage or otherwise, for the acquisition, construction, rehabilitation, repair, or maintenance of housing or otherwise withhold financing of housing from any person because of the race, color, religion, sex, ancestry, disability, national origin, or military status of any present or prospective owner, occupant, or user of the housing, or because of the racial composition of the neighborhood in which the housing is located, provided that the person, whether an

EQUAL HOUSING OPPORTUNITY

It Is Illegal To Discriminate Against Any Person Because of Race, Color, Religion, Sex, Familial Status, National Origin, Military Status, Disability or Ancestry

- **In the sale or rental of housing or residential lots**
- **In advertising the sale or rental of housing**
- **In the financing of housing**
- **In the provision of real estate brokerage services**

Blockbusting is also illegal.

The Broker and Sales Associates are licensed by the Ohio Department of Commerce, Division of Real Estate & Professional Licensing. The division may be contacted for inquiries and complaints and for information on the Real Estate Recovery Fund (Section 4735.12 of the Revised Code) as a source of satisfaction for unsatisfied civil judgments against a licensee.

Ohio Department of Commerce
Division of Real Estate &
Professional Licensing

77 S. High Street, 20th Floor
Columbus, OH 43215-6133
(614) 466-4100

www.com.ohio.gov/real

PROVIDED BY THE OHIO REAL ESTATE COMMISSION

Effective 3/25/2008

individual, corporation, or association of any type, lends money as one of the principal aspects or incident to his principal business and not only a part of the purchase price of an owner-occupied residence he is selling nor merely casually or occasionally to a relative or friend.

(4) Discriminate against any person in the terms or conditions of selling, transferring, assigning, renting, leasing or subleasing any housing, or in furnishing facilities, services, or privileges in connection with the ownership, occupancy, or use of any housing, including the sale of fire, extended coverage, or home owners' insurance, because of the race, color, religion, sex, ancestry, disability, national origin, or military status of any present or prospective owner, occupant, or user of the housing, or because of the racial composition of the neighborhood in which the housing is located.

(5) Discriminate against any person in the terms or conditions of any loan of money, whether or not secured by mortgage or otherwise, for the acquisition, construction, rehabilitation, repair, or maintenance of housing because of the race, color, religion, sex, ancestry, disability, national origin, or military status of any present or prospective owner, occupant or user of housing, or because of the racial composition of the neighborhood where housing is located.

(6) Refuse to consider without prejudice the combined income of both husband and wife for the purpose of extending mortgage credit to a married couple or either member thereof.

(7) Print, publish, or circulate any statement or advertisement relating to the sale, transfer, assignment, rental, lease, sublease, or acquisition of any housing or the loan of money, whether or not secured by mortgage or otherwise, for the acquisition, construction, rehabilitation, repair, or maintenance of housing which indicates any preference, limitation, specification, or discrimination based upon race, color, religion, sex, ancestry, disability, national origin, or military status, or an intention to make any such preference, limitation, specification, or discrimination.

(8) Except as otherwise provided in divisions (H)(8) of this section, make any inquiry, elicit any information, make or keep any record, or use any form of application containing questions or entries concerning race, color, religion, sex, ancestry, disability, national origin, or military status in connection with the sale or lease of any housing or the loan of any money, whether or not secured by mortgage or otherwise, for the acquisition, construction, rehabilitation, repair, or maintenance of housing. Any person may make inquiries, and make and keep records concerning race, color, religion, sex, ancestry, disability, national origin, or military status for the purpose of monitoring compliance with this chapter.

(9) Include in the transfer, rental, or lease of housing any restrictive covenant, or honor or exercise, or attempt to honor or exercise, any restrictive covenant, provided that the prior inclusion of a restrictive covenant in the chain of title shall not be deemed a violation of this provision.

(10) Induce or solicit or attempt to induce or solicit a housing listing, sale, or transaction by representing that a change has occurred or may occur with respect to the racial, religious, sexual, or ethnic composition of the block, neighborhood, or area in which the property is located, or induce or solicit or attempt to induce or solicit such sale or listing by representing that the

presence or anticipated presence of persons of any race, color, religion, sex, ancestry, disability, national origin, or military status in the area will or may have results such as:

(a) the lowering of property values

(b) a change in the racial, religious, sexual, or ethnic composition of the block, neighborhood, or area in which the property is located

(c) an increase in criminal or antisocial behavior in the area

(d) a decline in the quality of the schools serving the area

> (11) Deny any person access to or membership or participation in any multiple-listing service, real estate brokers' organization, or other service, organization, or facility relating to the business of selling or renting housing accommodations, or to discriminate against any person in the terms or conditions of such access, membership, or participation, on account of race, color, religion, sex, national origin, disability, ancestry, or military status.

(J) For any person to aid, abet, incite, compel, or coerce the doing of any act declared by this section to be unlawful discriminatory practice, or to obstruct or prevent any person from complying with sections 4112.01 to 4112.11 of the Revised Code, or any order issued hereunder, or to attempt directly or indirectly to commit any act declared by this section to be an unlawful discriminatory practice. For further reference, please see HB 321.

ANTI-DISCRIMINATION and FAIR HOUSING LAWS SUMMARIZED

	Civil Rights Act of 1866	Federal Fair Housing Act	Ohio Civil Rights Act	Federal Equal Credit Opportunity Act
Race	X	X	X	X
Color	X	X	X	X
Religion		X	X	X
Sex		X	X	X
National Origin		X	X	X
Ancestry	X		X	
Disability/Disability		X	X	
Familial Status		X	X	
Military Status			X	
Age				X
Marital Status				X
Receipt of Public Assistance				X
All property (Real + Personal)	X			
Only housing + land for housing		X		
Housing and ANY vacant land			X	
Exceptions (FSBO = For Sale By Owner)	NONE	1. FSBO 2. FSBO 4-plex 3. Religious Groups 4. Private Clubs	1. NO 2. NO 3. Relig. Grps 4. Private Clubs	
Statute of Limitations	Same as State (1 year in Ohio)	1 Year for HUD 2 Years for Court	1 Year	

TERMS TO REMEMBER

THESE WILL BE ON THE TEST IN ONE FORM OR ANOTHER!

Blockbusting: A prohibited act under federal and state law. It is defined as "inducing or attempting to induce, for profit, any person to sell or rent property based on representations made regarding entry into the neighborhood of persons of a particular race, color, religion, sex or national origin". Also known as panic peddling or panic selling.

Steering: The illegal practice of trying to influence a buyer's housing choice using racial, religious, ethnic, national origin, or ancestry factors. This includes showing only certain neighborhoods, or downgrading or slanting certain neighborhoods to influence minority buyers. This is illegal under federal and state law.

Redlining: The illegal practice of denying loans in certain areas of a community because of race, color, creed, religion, sex, national origin, familial status, and disability/disability. This occurs any time a decision is made that is not based on the buyers' qualifications. (It is also a practice used at times in the insurance industry.) This is illegal under federal and state law.

Fair Housing Information

	Civil Rights Act of 1866	Fair Housing Act: Civil Rights Act of 1968 **Title VIII As Amended by 1988 Fair Housing Act**
What the Laws Say	**Grant all citizens the same rights with regard to property as white citizens.**	Prohibits discrimination in the sale, rental, lease, or negotiations for real property based on race, color, religion, sex, disability, familial status, or national origin. Also prohibits discrimination in financing or provision of brokerage services.
Whom the Laws Protect	**Grant all citizens the same rights with regard to property as white citizens.**	Protects all persons (citizens or non-citizens) affected by discriminatory practices.
The Penalties the Court can Order	Injunctive relief, compensatory and punitive damages. Attorney's fees to the successful plaintiff.	Injunctive relief, compensatory and punitive damages which are not limited by the statute. Attorneys' fees may be allowed by the court or administrative judge to successful plaintiffs. Fines can be levied: * Up to $11,000 for first offense * Up to $27,500 for 2nd offense, * Up to $55,000 for 3rd or more offenses w/in 7 years
The Amount of Time Available To File a Complaint	*Determined by state law*	*One year after an alleged discriminatory housing practice has occurred or terminated to file a complaint with HUD or two (2) years after occurrence or the termination of an alleged discriminatory housing practice to file the complaint in federal district court.*
Basis for Filing Fair Housing Complaints	Discrimination against non-white citizens. Discrimination in the sale or rental of any type of property.	Discrimination based on race, color, religion, sex, disability, familial status, or national origin. Discrimination in the sale or rental of a dwelling.
How the Laws Are Enforced	**Civil actions can be brought in state or federal courts by persons injured by discriminatory conduct prohibited by the Act.**	The Attorney General can enforce this law where a "pattern or practice" of discrimination can be shown or where the issue presented is of general public importance. A person injured by an allegedly discriminatory practice can file a complaint with HUD or may file a suit in federal court without regard to the amount of damages in controversy. The secretary of HUD, on the secretary's own initiative, may file a complaint with HUD alleging a discriminatory housing practice. **Hearings on complaints filed with HUD may be transferred to the federal court for hearing in a civil action if requested by any party within twenty (20) days of receipt of service by the electing party.**
Types of Situations NOT Covered by the Laws	*No Exclusions*	Boarding houses with no more than three units and owner occupied. Transactions that do not involve the use of a broker or agent. **Non-commercial private clubs.**

Agency Law

Ohio Laws On Agency

The new Agency law in Ohio sets basic parameters for brokerage companies and permits individual companies to create their own agency policies. The state exam covers only statutory items and definitions, whereas your pre-licensing classes most likely discussed a variety of policy alternatives. That means the coverage on the state exam will probably be simpler than you expect.

This section covers the basic factual information you need to successfully answer questions on the exam about agency. At the end of this chapter, you will be tested on this basic information through a series of true/false questions. Finally, more complex, multiple-choice questions will demonstrate the actual type of questions you can expect on the exam.

Agent A broker is an agent of the principal client; salesperson licensees are agents of their broker; salesperson licensees are subagents of the principal client.

Client/Principal A person who has entered into an agency relationship with a licensee and with whom there is a written agency agreement.

Confidential Information All information the client directs to be confidential, which, if disclosed, would have an adverse effect on the client's position.

Customer Any third party with whom a licensee works.

In-Company Transaction Transaction in which the buyer and seller are both represented by the same brokerage.

Management-Level Licensee A licensee who is employed by or affiliated with a brokerage who has supervisory responsibility over other licensees.

Subagency An agency relationship in which a licensee acts for another licensee.

A dual agent must not:

(a) disclose information that is confidential or would have an adverse effect.

(b) advocate or negotiate on behalf of either party.

(c) suggest or recommend specific terms; **nor act in a biased manner for either party.**

Key Terms

Disclosure Forms

The agent or broker must present, and have signed by each seller and buyer, a **Consumer Guide to Agency Relationships** pamphlet or form that informs a buyer or seller what types of agency relationships a brokerage practices (i.e., sellers only, buyers only, split agency, dual agency) and how, if at all, a broker will divide a commission with another brokerage firm (i.e., co-op). This Consumer Guide to Agency Relationships form must be given to the respective parties as follows:

Seller/Landlord Disclosure

The Consumer Guide to Agency Relationships form must be given to and signed by a seller/landlord **prior to the showing or marketing of the seller's property.** Please note that it is not at the time the listing agreement is signed. While in real life that is certainly preferable, questions on the exam may require that you select a specific date for disclosure to occur. Read carefully for the date the first marketing or showing occurred.

Buyer/Tenant Disclosure

The Consumer Guide to Agency Relationships form must be given to and signed by a buyer/landlord **prior** to any of the following events:

*   Pre-qualifying to determine ability to purchase a specific property

*   Requesting financial information to determine a purchaser's price range

*   Showing a property, other than at an open-house.

*   Discussing making an offer

*   Submitting an offer

    √ **Note:** It is whichever one of these events occurs first. They may not happen in this order!

The Consumer Guide to Agency Relationships form must be presented prior to the earliest of the above events. If that event is by telephone, the Consumer Guide to Agency Relationship disclosure **may be made during the telephone conversation**, followed by having the buyer or seller sign the actual Consumer Guide to Agency Relationships form at the **first physical meeting following the verbal disclosure**.

    √ **Note:** The definition of "showing" specifically excludes open houses.

Additionally, each company is required to have a written company policy on agency. A summary of this policy must be provided, **upon request**, to all sellers, buyers, landlords, and tenants. The law does not prescribe a form for this disclosure other than that it must be in writing. The company policy would state who are management-level licensees, how confidential information will be protected, office policies on record keeping, etc.

Ohio has a two-page **Agency Disclosure Statement** form that incorporates all forms of agency that may exist between a broker and a client or a broker and a customer, (i.e., sellers, buyers, dual, split). It is to be given and signed by all sellers, purchasers, landlords, and tenants (for leases of more than 18 months), regardless of whether the real estate is residential or commercial. There are certain limited exceptions under the law; however, the exam does not deal with these exceptions, and they are not addressed here. **The Agency Disclosure Statement form must be signed by all parties to a real estate transaction prior to preparing or presenting an offer to purchase.**

Dual Agency/Disclosure

It is still permissible to act as a dual agent under Ohio Agency law. The circumstances when a dual agency may occur are as follows:

- A licensee who represents both the buyer and seller as clients in the same transaction

- A brokerage that represents both the buyer and seller as clients in the same transaction

- A management-level licensee who represents a client in an in-company transaction

- Two (2) licensees from the same brokerage, wherein one licensee is representing the buyer and another licensee (from the same brokerage) is representing the seller in the same transaction. Sometimes referred to as **Split** or **In-Company**.

When a licensee or brokerage will act as a dual agent, a disclosure must be made to the parties as soon as practicable after it is determined that a dual agency relationship exists. The disclosure is made using the same Ohio Agency Disclosure Statement form that is used for disclosing a singular agency (i.e., solely representing a seller or buyer), or a split agency.

A dual agent must:

- Treat both clients honestly

- Safeguard each party's confidential information

- Disclose latent material defects if known

- Provide information regarding lenders, inspectors, etc., if asked

- Provide marketing information if requested

- Prepare and present all offers as directed

- Assist both parties in completing the transaction if requested

Representation/Subagency

The previous presumption of subagency, that every licensee represents the seller, has been eliminated under Ohio Agency law.

Now, when a sales licensee enters into a listing agreement, only that licensee and the broker are presumed under Ohio law to be representing the seller. Similarly, the same is true if a sales agent enters into a buyer brokerage agreement, in that only the broker and that specific agent are the ones presumed under Ohio law to be representing the buyer. Your own company policy, however, could say that if one agent in the firm signed a seller or buyer; then all agents in the firm will also represent that seller or buyer, but that would be because of your company policy, not what the Ohio law presumes.

One alternative permitted by Ohio law is the **split agent**, sometimes call **In-Company Transactions**. In **Split Agency,** an agent in the firm who actually takes a listing will be designated to represent that seller; and, if another agent in the same firm should sign a buyer, then that agent will be designated to represent that buyer. The broker will be a dual agent representing both seller and buyer, limited to a very intermediary role in the transaction. This is a form of dual agency but places a great responsibility on the broker to maintain the confidentiality of information possessed by the both salespersons.

Auctions

A licensee selling property at auction must verbally disclose, prior to the auction, that he represents the seller. The Ohio Agency Disclosure Statement must then be provided to the successful bidder prior to the signing of a purchase agreement.

Changes in Relationship

Any time your agency relationship changes, that change must be disclosed to the buyer or seller in writing. They must consent to the change. If they do not, they have the right to seek representation from another licensee. This could be a licensee within your organization or in another company, depending on company policy. Whether they owe a commission would be a matter of company policy and depend on individual contracts.

Material Relationships

A requirement of being a dual agent is that the licensee act in an **unbiased manner**. This becomes difficult if the licensee has a material relationship with anyone involved in the transaction. An example would be when one party is a family member. All material relationships with the buyer, seller, or real estate licensee must be disclosed in writing. Space is provided in the Ohio Agency Disclosure Statement in the "Dual Agency" section of the form.

*Copies of the Ohio Division of Real Estate's suggested **Consumer Guide to Agency Relationships** (Exhibits 1-5) and the state-mandated **Agency Disclosure Statement** form (Exhibit 6) follow:*

CONSUMER GUIDE TO AGENCY RELATIONSHIPS

(Exclusive Seller Agency - Model Policy)

Brokerage Name

We are pleased you have selected (brokerage) to help you with your real estate needs. Whether you are selling, buying or leasing real estate, (brokerage) can provide you with expertise and assistance. Because this may be the largest financial transaction you will enter into, it is important to understand the role of the agents and brokers with whom you are working. Below is some information that explains the various services that agents can offer and their options for working with you.

For more information on agency law in Ohio, contact the Ohio Division of Real Estate & Professional Licensing at (614) 466-4100, or online at www.com.ohio.gov/real.

Representing the Sellers

Most sellers of real estate choose to list their home for sale with a real estate brokerage. When they do so, they sign a listing agreement that authorizes the brokerage and the listing agent to represent their interests. As the seller's agent, the brokerage and listing agent must: follow the seller's lawful instructions, be loyal to the seller, promote the seller's best interests, disclose material facts to the seller, maintain confidential information, act with reasonable skill and care, and account for any money they handle in the transaction. In rare circumstances, a listing broker may offer "subagency" to other brokerages, which would also represent the seller's interests and owe the seller these same duties.

Representing Buyers

When purchasing real estate, buyers usually choose to work with a real estate agent as well. Often the buyers want to be represented in the transaction. This is referred to as buyer's agency. A brokerage and agent that agree to represent a buyer's interest in a transaction must: follow the buyer's lawful instructions, be loyal to the buyer, promote the buyer's best interests, disclose material facts to the buyer, maintain confidential information, and account for any money they handle in the transaction.

Dual Agency

Occasionally, the same agent and brokerage that represent the seller also represent the buyer. This is referred to as dual agency. When a brokerage and its agents become "dual agents," they must maintain a neutral position between the buyer and the seller. They may not advocate the position of one client over the best interests of the other client, or disclose any personal or confidential information to the other party without written consent.

Representing Both the Buyer & Seller

On occasion, the buyer and seller will each be represented by two different agents from the same brokerage. In this case, the agents may each represent the best interest of their respective clients. Or, depending on company policy, the agents may both act as dual agents and remain neutral in the transaction. When either of the above occurs, the brokerage will be considered a dual agent. As a dual agent, the brokerage and its managers will maintain a neutral position and cannot advocate for the position of one client over another. The brokerage will also protect the confidentiality of all parties.

For more information on agency law in Ohio, contact the Ohio Division of Real Estate & Professional Licensing at (614) 466-4100, or online at www.com.ohio.gov/real.

Working With (brokerage)

(Brokerage) only represents seller. It does not represent buyers of real estate. Therefore, (brokerage) will never act as a dual agent representing both parties in a transaction. Instead, it will only act as the seller's agent in the sale of real estate.

Even though (brokerage) only lists properties for sellers, it can still work with buyers as customers. (Brokerage) can provide buyers with non-confidential information and write offers at the buyer's direction, but will not act as the agent of these buyers. Instead, such buyers will represent their own best interests.

It is also important for buyers to understand that because the listing agent has a duty of full disclosure to the seller, buyers should not share any information with the listing agent that they would not want the seller to know.

Working With Other Brokerages

When (brokerage) lists property for sale, it also cooperates with, and offers compensation to, other brokerages that represent buyers. (Brokerage) does reserve the right, in some instances, to vary the compensation it offers to other brokerages. As a seller, you should understand that just because (brokerage) shares a fee with a brokerage representing the buyer, it does not mean that you will be represented by that buyer's brokerage. Instead, that company will be looking out for the buyer and (brokerage) will be representing your interests.

Fair Housing Statement

It is illegal, pursuant to the Ohio Fair Housing Law, division (H) of Section 4112.02 of the Revised Code and the Federal Fair Housing Law, 42 U.S.C.A. 3601, as amended, to refuse to sell, transfer, assign, rent, lease, sublease or finance housing accommodations, refuse to negotiate for the sale or rental of housing accommodations, or otherwise deny or make unavailable housing accommodations because of race, color, religion, sex, familial status as defined in Section 4112.01 of the Revised Code, ancestry, military status as defined in that section, disability as defined in that section, or national origin or to so discriminate in advertising the sale or rental of housing, in the financing of housing, or in the provision of real estate brokerage services. It is also illegal, for profit, to induce or attempt to induce a person to sell or rent a dwelling by representations regarding the entry into the neighborhood of a person or persons belonging to one of the protected classes.

We hope you find this information to be helpful to you as you begin your real estate transaction. When you are ready to enter into a transaction, you will be given an Agency Disclosure Statement that specifically identifies the role of the agents and brokerages. Please ask questions if there is anything you do not understand.

Because it is important that you have this information, Ohio law requires that we ask you to sign below to acknowledge receipt of this pamphlet. Your signature will not obligate you to work with our company if you do not choose to do so.

_____   _____
Name   (Please Print)   Name   (Please Print)

_____   _____
Signature   Date   Signature   Date

Revised: 9/2011

CONSUMER GUIDE TO AGENCY RELATIONSHIPS

(Exclusive Buyer Agency Only – Model Policy)

Brokerage Name

We are pleased you have selected (brokerage) to help you with your real estate needs. Whether you are selling, buying or leasing real estate, (brokerage) can provide you with expertise and assistance. Because this may be the largest financial transaction you will enter into, it is important to understand the role of the agents and brokers with whom you are working. Below is some information that explains the various services that agents can offer and their options for working with you:

Representing the Sellers
Most sellers of real estate choose to list their home for sale with a real estate brokerage. When they do so, they sign a listing agreement that authorizes the brokerage and the listing agent to represent their interests. As the seller's agent, the brokerage and listing agent must: follow the seller's lawful instructions, be loyal to the seller, promote the seller's best interests, disclose material facts to the seller, maintain confidential information, act with reasonable skill and care, and account for any money they handle in the transaction. In rare circumstances, a listing broker may offer "subagency" to other brokerages, which would also represent the seller's interests and owe the seller these same duties.

Representing Buyers
When purchasing real estate, buyers usually choose to work with a real estate agent as well. Often the buyers want to be represented in the transaction. This is referred to as buyer's agency. A brokerage and agent that agree to represent a buyer's interest in a transaction must: follow the buyer's lawful instructions, be loyal to the buyer, promote the buyer's best interests, disclose material facts to the buyer, maintain confidential information, and account for any money they handle in the transaction.

Dual Agency
Occasionally, the same agent and brokerage that represent the seller also represent the buyer. This is referred to as dual agency. When a brokerage and its agents become "dual agents," they must maintain a neutral position in the transaction. They may not advocate the position of one client over the best interests of the other client, or disclose any confidential information to the other party without written consent.

Representing Both the Buyer & Seller
On occasion, the buyer and seller will each be represented by two different agents from the same brokerage. In this case, the agents may each represent the best interest of their respective clients. Or, depending on company policy, the agents may both act as dual agents and remain neutral in the transaction. When either of the above occurs, the brokerage will be considered a dual agent. As a dual agent, the brokerage and its managers will maintain a neutral position and cannot advocate for the position of one client over another. The brokerage will also protect the confidentiality of all parties.

For more information on agency law in Ohio, contact the Ohio Division of Real Estate & Professional Licensing at (614) 466-4100, or online at www.com.ohio.gov/real.

Working With (brokerage)

(Brokerage) only represents buyers. It does not represent sellers or list property for sale. Therefore, (brokerage) will never act as a dual agent representing both parties in a transaction. Instead, it will only act as the buyer's agent in the purchase of real estate.

When acting as a buyer's agent, (brokerage) will seek its compensation from the listing broker. If the property is not listed with any broker, or the listing broker does not offer compensation, the brokerage will attempt to negotiate for a seller-paid fee. However, even if the listing broker or seller pays us, (brokerage) still represents only the buyer.

If (brokerage) is not compensated by the listing broker or the seller, its compensation will be paid by the buyer, pursuant to a written agreement with the buyer.

Fair Housing Statement

It is illegal, pursuant to the Ohio Fair Housing Law, division (H) of Section 4112.02 of the Revised Code and the Federal Fair Housing Law, 42 U.S.C.A. 3601, as amended, to refuse to sell, transfer, assign, rent, lease, sublease or finance housing accommodations, refuse to negotiate for the sale or rental of housing accommodations, or otherwise deny or make unavailable housing accommodations because of race, color, religion, sex, familial status as defined in Section 4112.01 of the Revised Code, ancestry, military status as defined in that section, disability as defined in that section, or national origin or to so discriminate in advertising the sale or rental of housing, in the financing of housing, or in the provision of real estate brokerage services. It is also illegal, for profit, to induce or attempt to induce a person to sell or rent a dwelling by representations regarding the entry into the neighborhood of a person or persons belonging to one of the protected classes.

We hope you find this information to be helpful to you as you begin your real estate transaction. When you are ready to enter into a transaction, you will be given an Agency Disclosure Statement that specifically identifies the role of the agents and brokerages. Please ask questions if there is anything you do not understand.

Because it is important that you have this information Ohio law requires that we ask you to sign below to acknowledge receipt of this consumer guide. Your signature will not obligate you to work with our company if you do not choose to do so.

_____
Name   (Please Print)

_____
Signature   Date

_____
Name   (Please Print)

_____
Signature   Date

CONSUMER GUIDE TO AGENCY RELATIONSHIPS

(Split Agency but No Dual Agency– Model Policy)

Brokerage Name

We are pleased you have selected (brokerage) to help you with your real estate needs. Whether you are selling, buying or leasing real estate, (brokerage) can provide you with expertise and assistance. Because this may be the largest financial transaction you will enter into, it is important to understand the role of the agents and brokers with whom you are working. Below is some information that explains the various services that agents can offer and their options for working with you.

Representing the Sellers
Most sellers of real estate choose to list their home for sale with a real estate brokerage. When they do so, they sign a listing agreement that authorizes the brokerage and the listing agent to represent their interests. As the seller's agent, the brokerage and listing agent must: follow the seller's lawful instructions, be loyal to the seller, promote the seller's best interests, disclose material facts to the seller, maintain confidential information, act with reasonable skill and care, and account for any money they handle in the transaction. In rare circumstances, a listing broker may offer "subagency" to other brokerages, which would also represent the seller's interests and owe the seller these same duties.

Representing Buyers
When purchasing real estate, buyers usually choose to work with a real estate agent as well. Often the buyers want to be represented in the transaction. This is referred to as buyer's agency. A brokerage and agent that agree to represent a buyer's interest in a transaction must: follow the buyer's lawful instructions, be loyal to the buyer, promote the buyer's best interests, disclose material facts to the buyer, maintain confidential information, and account for any money they handle in the transaction.

Dual Agency
Occasionally, the same agent and brokerage that represent the seller also represent the buyer. This is referred to as dual agency. When a brokerage and its agents become "dual agents," they must maintain a neutral position between the buyer and the seller. They may not advocate the position of one client over the best interests of the other client, or disclose any personal or confidential information to the other party without written consent.

Representing Both the Buyer & Seller
On occasion, the buyer and seller will each be represented by two different agents from the same brokerage. In this case, the agents may each represent the best interest of their respective clients. Or, depending on company policy, the agents may both act as dual agents and remain neutral in the transaction. When either of the above occurs, the brokerage will be considered a dual agent. As a dual agent, the brokerage and its managers will maintain a neutral position and cannot advocate for the position of one client over another. The brokerage will also protect the confidentiality of all parties.

For more information on agency law in Ohio, contact the Ohio Division of Real Estate & Professional Licensing at (614) 466-4100, or online at www.com.ohio.gov/real.

Working With (brokerage)

(Brokerage) does offer representation to both buyers and sellers. Therefore, the potential exists for one agent to represent a buyer who wishes to purchase property listed with another agent in our company. If this occurs, each agent will represent their own client, but (brokerage) and its managers will act as a dual agent.

This means the brokerage and its managers will maintain a neutral position and not take any actions that will favor one side over the other. However, (brokerage) will still supervise both agents to assure that their clients are being fully represented.

While it is the policy of (brokerage) to allow a buyer and seller in the same transaction to be represented by two agents in our brokerage, it does not permit one agent to represent both parties. Therefore, a listing agent working directly with a buyer will represent only the seller's interests. The agent will still be able to provide the buyer with non-confidential information, prepare and present offers at their direction and assist the buyer in the financing and closing process. However, the buyer will represent their own interests. Because the listing agent has a duty of full disclosure to the seller, a buyer in this situation should not share any information with the listing agent that they would not want the seller to know. If a buyer wishes to be represented, another agent in (brokerage) can be appointed to act as their agent or they can seek representation from another brokerage.

Working With Other Brokerages

(Brokerage) does offer representation to both buyers and sellers. When (brokerage) lists property for sale, it also cooperates with, and offers compensation to, other brokerages that represent buyers. (Brokerage) does reserve the right, in some instances, to vary the compensation it offers to other brokerages. As a seller, you should understand that just because (brokerage) shares a fee with a brokerage representing the buyer, it does not mean that you will be represented by that buyer's brokerage. Instead, that company will be looking out for the buyer and (brokerage) will be representing your interests.

When acting as a buyer's agent, (brokerage) also accepts compensation offered by the listing broker. If the property is not listed with any broker, or the listing broker does not offer compensation, we will attempt to negotiate for a seller-paid fee.

Fair Housing Statement: It is illegal, pursuant to the Ohio Fair Housing Law, division (H) of Section 4112.02 of the Revised Code and the Federal Fair Housing Law, 42 U.S.C.A. 3601, as amended, to refuse to sell, transfer, assign, rent, lease, sublease or finance housing accomodations, refuse to negotiate for the sale or rental of housing accommodations, or otherwise deny or make unavailable housing accomodations because of race, color, religion, sex, familial status as defined in Section 4112.01 of the Revised Code, ancestry, military status as defined in that section, disability as defined in that section, or national origin or to so discriminate in advertising the sale or rental of housing, in the financing of housing, or in the provision of real estate brokerage services. It is also illegal, for profit, to induce or attempt to induce a person to sell or rent a dwelling by representations regarding the entry into the neighborhood of a person or persons belonging to one of the protected classes. (Effective: 9/29/11)

We hope you find this information to be helpful to you as you begin your real estate transaction. When you are ready to enter into a transaction, you will be given an Agency Disclosure Statement that specifically identifies the role of the agents and brokerages. Please ask questions if there is anything you do not understand.

Because it is important that you have this information, Ohio law requires that we ask you to sign below to acknowledge receipt of this pamphlet. Your signature will not obligate you to work with our company if you do not choose to do so.

_____ (Please Print)   _____ (Please Print)
Name   Name

_____   _____
Signature   Date   Signature   Date

CONSUMER GUIDE TO AGENCY RELATIONSHIPS

(Split Agency & Dual Agency – Model Policy)

Brokerage Name

We are pleased you have selected (brokerage) to help you with your real estate needs. Whether you are selling, buying or leasing real estate (brokerage) can provide you with expertise and assistance. Because this may be the largest financial transaction you will enter into, it is important to understand the role of the agents and brokers with whom you are working. Below is some information that explains the various services agents can offer and their options for working with you:

Representing the Sellers
Most sellers of real estate choose to list their home for sale with a real estate brokerage. When they do so, they sign a listing agreement that authorizes the brokerage and the listing agent to represent their interests. As the seller's agent, the brokerage and listing agent must: follow the seller's lawful instructions, be loyal to the seller, promote the seller's best interests, disclose material facts to the seller, maintain confidential information, act with reasonable skill and care and, account for any money they handle in the transaction. In rare circumstances a listing broker may offer "subagency" to other brokerages which would also represent the seller's interests and owe the seller these same duties.

Representing Buyers
When purchasing real estate, buyers usually choose to work with a real estate agent as well. Often the buyers want to be represented in the transaction. This is referred to as buyer's agency. A brokerage and agent that agree to represent a buyer's interest in a transaction must: follow the buyer's lawful instructions, be loyal to the buyer, promote the buyer's best interests, disclose material facts to the buyer, maintain confidential information and, account for any money they handle in the transaction.

Dual Agency
Occasionally the same agent and brokerage who represents the seller also represents the buyer. This is referred to as dual agency. When a brokerage and its agents become "dual agents", they must maintain a neutral position in the transaction. They may not advocate the position of one client over the best interests of the other client, or disclose any confidential information to the other party without written consent.

Representing Both the Buyer & Seller
On occasion, the buyer and seller will each be represented by two different agents from the same brokerage. In this case the agents may each represent the best interest of their respective clients. Or, depending on company policy, the agents may both act as dual agents and remain neutral in the transaction. When either of the above occurs, the brokerage will be considered a dual agent. As a dual agent the brokerage and its managers will maintain a neutral position and cannot advocate for the position of one client over another. The brokerage will also protect the confidentiality of all parties.

For more information on agency law in Ohio you can also contact the Ohio Division of Real Estate & Professional Licensing at (614) 466-4100, or on their website www.com.state.oh.us.

Working With (brokerage)

(brokerage) does offer rep resentation to both buy ers and sellers. Therefore the potential exists for one a gent to represent a buyer who wishes to purchase property listed with another agent in our com pany. If this occu rs each agent will represent their own client, but (brokerage) and its managers will act as a dual agent. This means the brokerage and its manage rs will maintain a neutral position and not take any actions that will favor one side over the other. (brokerage) will still supervise both agents to assure that their respective clients are being fully represented and will protect the parties' confidential information.

In the event that both the buyer and seller are represented by the same agent, that agent and (brokerage) will act as a dual agent but only if both parties agree . As a dual agen t they will treat both parties honestly, prepare and present offers at the direction of the parties, an d help the par ties fulfill the terms of an y contract. They will not, however, disclose any confidential inform ation that would place one party at an advantage over the other or ad vocate or negotiate to the detriment of either party.

If dual agency occurs you will be asked to consent to that in writing. If you do not agree to your agent acting as a dual agent, you can ask that another agent in ou r company be assigned t o represent you or you can seek representation from another brokerage.

As a buyer you m ay also choose to represent yourself on properties (brokerage) has listed. In that instance (brokerage) will represent the seller and you would represent your own best interests. Because the listing agent has a duty of full disclosure to the seller you should not share any information with the listing agent that you would not want the seller to know.

Working With Other Brokerages

When (brokerage) lists property for sale it also cooperates with, a nd offers compensation to, other brokerages that represent buyers. (Brokerage) does reserve the right, in some insta nces, to vary the compensation it offers to other brokerages. As a seller, you should understand that just because (brokerage) shares a fee with a brokerage representing the buyer, it does not m ean that you will be represented by that brokerage. Instead that co mpany will be looking out for the buy er and (brokerage) will be representing your interests. When acting as a buyer's agent, (brokerage) also accepts compensation offered by the listing broker. If the property is not listed with any broker, or the listing broker does not offer compensation, we will attempt to negotiate for a seller-paid fee.

Fair Housing Statement

It is illegal, pursuant to the Ohio Fair Housing Law, division (H) of Section 4112.02 of the Revised Code and the Federal Fair Housing Law, 42 U.S.C.A. 3601, as amended, to refuse to sell, transfer, assign, rent, lease, sublease or finance housing accommodations, refuse to negotiate for the sale or rental of housing accommodations, or otherwise deny or make unavailable housing accommodations because of race, color, religion, sex, familial status as defined in Section 4112.01 of the Revised Code, ancestry, military status as defined in that section, disability as defined in that section, or national origin or to so discriminate in advertising the sale or rental of housing, in the financing of housing, or in the provision of real estate brokerage services. It is also illegal, for profit, to induce or attempt to induce a person to sell or rent a dwelling by representations regarding the entry into the neighborhood of a person or persons belonging to one of the protected classes. (Effective: 9/29/11)

We hope you find this inf ormation to be helpful to you as you begin your real estate transaction. When y ou are ready to enter into a transaction, y ou will be given an Agency Disclosure Statement that specifically identifies the role of the agents and brokerages. Pl ease ask questions if there is anything you do not unders tand. Because it is important that you have this information Ohio law requires that we ask you to sign below, acknowledging receipt of this consumer guide. Your signature will not obligate you to work with our company if you do not choose to do so.

_____   _____
Name   (Please Print)   Name   (Please Print)

_____   _____
Signature   Date   Signature   Date

CONSUMER GUIDE TO AGENCY RELATIONSHIPS

(Dual Agency In All In House Transactions – Model Policy)

Brokerage Name

We are pleased you have selected (brokerage) to help you with your real estate needs. Whether you are selling, buying or leasing real estate, (brokerage) can provide you with expertise and assistance. Because this may be the largest financial transaction you will enter into, it is important to understand the role of the agents and brokers with whom you are working. Below is some information that explains the various services that agents can offer and their options for working with you:

Representing the Sellers
Most sellers of real estate choose to list their home for sale with a real estate brokerage. When they do so, they sign a listing agreement that authorizes the brokerage and the listing agent to represent their interests. As the seller's agent, the brokerage and listing agent must: follow the seller's lawful instructions, be loyal to the seller, promote the seller's best interests, disclose material facts to the seller, maintain confidential information, act with reasonable skill and care, and account for any money they handle in the transaction. In rare circumstances, a listing broker may offer "subagency" to other brokerages, which would also represent the seller's interests and owe the seller these same duties.

Representing Buyers
When purchasing real estate, buyers usually choose to work with a real estate agent as well. Often the buyers want to be represented in the transaction. This is referred to as buyer's agency. A brokerage and agent that agree to represent a buyer's interest in a transaction must: follow the buyer's lawful instructions, be loyal to the buyer, promote the buyer's best interests, disclose material facts to the buyer, maintain confidential information, and account for any money they handle in the transaction.

Dual Agency
Occasionally, the same agent and brokerage that represent the seller also represent the buyer. This is referred to as dual agency. When a brokerage and its agents become "dual agents," they must maintain a neutral position in the transaction. They may not advocate the position of one client over the best interests of the other client, or disclose any confidential information to the other party without written consent.

Representing Both the Buyer & Seller
On occasion, the buyer and seller will each be represented by two different agents from the same brokerage. In this case, the agents may each represent the best interest of their respective clients. Or, depending on company policy, the agents may both act as dual agents and remain neutral in the transaction. When either of the above occurs, the brokerage will be considered a dual agent. As a dual agent, the brokerage and its managers will maintain a neutral position and cannot advocate for the position of one client over another. The brokerage will also protect the confidentiality of all parties.

For more information on agency law in Ohio, contact the Ohio Division of Real Estate & Professional Licensing at (614) 466-4100, or online at www.com.ohio.gov/real.

Working With (brokerage)

(Brokerage) does represent both buyers and sellers. When (brokerage) lists property for sale, all agents in the brokerage represent the seller. Likewise, when a buyer is represented by a (brokerage) agent, all of the agents represent that buyer. Therefore, when a buyer represented by a (brokerage) agent wishes to purchase property listed by our company, the agent(s) involved act as dual agents. This is true whether one agent is representing both parties or two separate agents are involved.

In the event that both the buyer and seller are represented by (brokerage) agents, these agents and (brokerage) will act as a dual agent but only if both parties agree. As a dual agent, they will treat both parties honestly, prepare and present offers at the direction of the parties, and help the parties fulfill the terms of any contract. They will not, however, disclose any confidential information that will place one party at an advantage over the other or advocate or negotiate to the detriment of either party.

If dual agency occurs, you will be asked to consent to that in writing. If you do not agree to your agent acting as a dual agent, you can seek representation from another brokerage.

As a buyer, you may also choose to represent yourself on properties (brokerage) has listed. In that instance, (brokerage) will represent the seller and you would represent your own best interests. Because the listing agent has a duty of full disclosure to the seller, you should not share any information with the listing agent that you would not want the seller to know.

Working With Other Brokerages

(Brokerage) does offer representation to both buyers and sellers. When (brokerage) lists property for sale, it also cooperates with, and offers compensation to, other brokerages that represent buyers. (Brokerage) does reserve the right, in some instances, to vary the compensation it offers to other brokerages. As a seller, you should understand that just because (brokerage) shares a fee with a brokerage representing the buyer, it does not mean that you will be represented by that buyer's brokerage. Instead, that company will be looking out for the buyer and (brokerage) will be representing your interests.

When acting as a buyer's agent, (brokerage) also accepts compensation offered by the listing broker. If the property is not listed with any broker, or the listing broker does not offer compensation, we will attempt to negotiate for a seller-paid fee.

Fair Housing Statement

It is illegal, pursuant to the Ohio Fair Housing Law, division (H) of Section 4112.02 of the Revised Code and the Federal Fair Housing Law, 42 U.S.C.A. 3601, as amended, to refuse to sell, transfer, assign, rent, lease, sublease or finance housing accommodations, refuse to negotiate for the sale or rental of housing accommodations, or otherwise deny or make unavailable housing accommodations because of race, color, religion, sex, familial status as defined in Section 4112.01 of the Revised Code, ancestry, military status as defined in that section, disability as defined in that section, or national origin or to so discriminate in advertising the sale or rental of housing, in the financing of housing, or in the provision of real estate brokerage services. It is also illegal, for profit, to induce or attempt to induce a person to sell or rent a dwelling by representations regarding the entry into the neighborhood of a person or persons belonging to one of the protected classes. (Effective: 9/29/11)

We hope you find this information to be helpful to you as you begin your real estate transaction. When you are ready to enter into a transaction, you will be given an Agency Disclosure Statement that specifically identifies the role of the agents and brokerages. Please ask questions if there is anything you do not understand.

Because it is important that you have this information, Ohio law requires that we ask you to sign below to acknowledge receipt of this pamphlet. Your signature will not obligate you to work with our company if you do not choose to do so.

Name	(Please Print)	Name	(Please Print)

Signature	Date	Signature	Date

AGENCY DISCLOSURE STATEMENT

The real estate agent who is providing you with this form is required to do so by Ohio law. You will not be bound to pay the agent or the agent's brokerage by merely signing this form. Instead, the purpose of this form is to confirm that you have been advised of the role of the agent(s) in the transaction proposed below. (For purposes of this form, the term "seller" includes a landlord and the term "buyer" includes a tenant.)

Property Address: _____

Buyer(s): _____

Seller(s): _____

I. TRANSACTION INVOLVING TWO AGENTS IN TWO DIFFERENT BROKERAGES

The buyer will be represented by _____, and _____.
AGENT(S)   BROKERAGE

The seller will be represented by _____, and _____.
AGENT(S)   BROKERAGE

II. TRANSACTION INVOLVING TWO AGENTS IN THE SAME BROKERAGE

If two agents in the real estate brokerage _____
represent both the buyer and the seller, check the following relationship that will apply:

☐ Agent(s)_____ work(s) for the buyer and
Agent(s)_____ work(s) for the seller. Unless personally involved in the transaction, the broker and managers will be "dual agents", which is further explained on the back of this form. As dual agents they will maintain a neutral position in the transaction and they will protect all parties' confidential information.

☐ Every agent in the brokerage represents every "client" of the brokerage. Therefore, agents _____ and _____ will be working for both the buyer and seller as "dual agents". Dual agency is explained on the back of this form. As dual agents they will maintain a neutral position in the transaction and they will protect all parties' confidential information. Unless indicated below, neither the agent(s) nor the brokerage acting as a dual agent in this transaction has a personal, family or business relationship with either the buyer or seller. *If such a relationship does exist, explain:* _____.

III. TRANSACTION INVOLVING ONLY ONE REAL ESTATE AGENT

Agent(s) _____ and real estate brokerage _____ will

☐ be "dual agents" representing both parties in this transaction in a neutral capacity. Dual agency is further explained on the back of this form. As dual agents they will maintain a neutral position in the transaction and they will protect all parties' confidential information. Unless indicated below, neither the agent(s) nor the brokerage acting as a dual agent in this transaction has a personal, family or business relationship with either the buyer or seller. *If such a relationship does exist, explain*: _____.

☐ represent only the (*check one*) ☐ **seller** or ☐ **buyer** in this transaction as a client. The other party is not represented and agrees to represent his/her own best interest. Any information provided the agent may be disclosed to the agent's client.

CONSENT

I (we) consent to the above relationships as we enter into this real estate transaction. If there is a dual agency in this transaction, I (we) acknowledge reading the information regarding dual agency explained on the back of this form.

_____   _____
BUYER/TENANT   *DATE*   *SELLER/LANDLORD*   *DATE*

_____   _____
BUYER/TENANT   *DATE*   *SELLER/LANDLORD*   *DATE*

DUAL AGENCY

Ohio law permits a real estate agent and brokerage to represent both the seller and buyer in a real estate transaction as long as this is disclosed to both parties and they both agree. This is known as dual agency. As a dual agent, a real estate agent and brokerage represent two clients whose interests are, or at times could be, different or adverse. For this reason, the dual agent(s) may not be able to advocate on behalf of the client to the same extent the agent may have if the agent represented only one client.

As a dual agent, the agent(s) and brokerage shall:
- Treat both clients honestly;
- Disclose latent (not readily observable) material defects to the purchaser, if known by the agent(s) or brokerage;
- Provide information regarding lenders, inspectors and other professionals, if requested;
- Provide market information available from a property listing service or public records, if requested;
- Prepare and present all offers and counteroffers at the direction of the parties;
- Assist both parties in completing the steps necessary to fulfill the terms of any contract, if requested.

As a dual agent, the agent(s) and brokerage shall not:
- Disclose information that is confidential, or that would have an adverse effect on one party's position in the transaction, unless such disclosure is authorized by the client or required by law;
- Advocate or negotiate on behalf of either the buyer or seller;
- Suggest or recommend specific terms, including price, or disclose the terms or price a buyer is willing to offer or that a seller is willing to accept;
- Engage in conduct that is contrary to the instructions of either party and may not act in a biased manner on behalf of one party.

Compensation: Unless agreed otherwise, the brokerage will be compensated per the agency agreement.

Management Level Licensees: Generally the broker and managers in a brokerage also represent the interests of any buyer or seller represented by an agent affiliated with that brokerage. Therefore, if both buyer and seller are represented by agents in the same brokerage, the broker and manager are dual agents. There are two exceptions to this. The first is where the broker or manager is personally representing one of the parties. The second is where the broker or manager is selling or buying his own real estate. These exceptions only apply if there is another broker or manager to supervise the other agent involved in the transaction.

Responsibilities of the Parties: The duties of the agent and brokerage in a real estate transaction do not relieve the buyer and seller from the responsibility to protect their own interests. The buyer and seller are advised to carefully read all agreements to assure that they adequately express their understanding of the transaction. The agent and brokerage are qualified to advise on real estate matters. IF LEGAL OR TAX ADVICE IS DESIRED, YOU SHOULD CONSULT THE APPROPRIATE PROFESSIONAL.

Consent: By signing on the reverse side, you acknowledge that you have read and understand this form and are giving your voluntary, informed consent to the agency relationship disclosed. If you do not agree to the agent(s) and/or brokerage acting as a dual agent, you are not required to consent to this agreement and you may either request a separate agent in the brokerage to be appointed to represent your interests or you may terminate your agency relationship and obtain representation from another brokerage.

Any questions regarding the role or responsibilities of the brokerage or its agents should be directed to an attorney or to:
Ohio Department of Commerce
Division of Real Estate & Professional Licensing
77 S. High Street, 20th Floor
Columbus, OH 43215-6133
(614) 466-4100

EQUAL HOUSING OPPORTUNITY

	OHIO DEPARTMENT OF COMMERCE Division of Real Estate and Professional Licensing	**WAIVER OF DUTIES STATEMENT** Pursuant to ORC 4735.621 *To Be Used when Certain Duties are Waived by the Client*

REQUIRED DUTIES:

After entering into an agency relationship, a real estate licensee (meaning a licensed broker or salesperson) is considered a "fiduciary" of the client. This means the licensee will use his or her best efforts to further the interests of the client. Under Ohio law, these fiduciary duties <u>may not</u> be waived. The client's real estate licensee must:

- Exercise reasonable skill and care in representing the client and carrying out the responsibilities of the agency relationship;
- Perform the terms of any written agency agreement;
- Follow any lawful instructions of the client;
- Be loyal to the interest of the client;
- Comply with all requirements of Ohio real estate licensing laws and other applicable statutes, rules, and regulations, including state and federal fair housing laws
- Disclose any material facts of the transaction of which the licensee is or should be aware
- Advise the client to obtain expert advice related to material matters when necessary or appropriate;
- Account in a timely manner for all moneys and property received in which the client has or may have an interest;
- Keep all confidential information confidential, unless permitted to disclose the information pursuant to ORC 4735.74(B). This includes the duty to not disclose confidential information to any licensee who is not an agent of the client.

DUTIES THAT <u>MAY</u> BE WAIVED:

Under Ohio law, a real estate licensee is required to perform additional duties for his or her client <u>unless these duties are waived by the client</u>. By signing below, the client agrees that the real estate licensee will <u>not</u> perform the duties initialed (only initial the duties waived)

Sellers may waive:	Initial If Waived:	
• Seeking a purchase offer at a price and with terms acceptable to the seller	_____	_____
• Accepting delivery of and presenting any purchase offer to the seller in a timely manner, even if the property is subject to a contract of sale, lease, or letter of intent to lease	_____	_____
• Answering the seller's questions and providing information to the seller regarding any offers or counteroffers	_____	_____
• Assisting the seller in developing, communicating, and presenting offers or counteroffers	_____	_____
• Answering the seller's questions regarding the steps the seller must take to fulfill the terms of any contract (within the scope of knowledge required for real estate licensure)	_____	_____
Buyers may waive:		
• Seeking a property at a price and with purchase or lease terms acceptable to the buyer	_____	_____
• Presenting any offer to purchase or lease to the seller or the seller's agent in a timely manner and accepting delivery of and presenting any counteroffers to the buyer	_____	_____
• Answering the buyer's questions and providing information to the buyer regarding any offers or counteroffers	_____	_____
• Assisting the buyer in developing, communicating, and presenting offers or counteroffers	_____	_____
• Answering the buyer's questions regarding the steps the buyer must take to fulfill the terms of any contract (within the scope of knowledge required for real estate licensure)	_____	_____

Agreement to Waive

By signing below, I agree that the real estate licensee who represents me will not perform the duties that are initialed above. I also understand that in any proposed real estate transaction, no other real estate licensee is required to perform the waived duties unless I subsequently hire them to do so, and realize that I may need to hire other professionals such as an attorney.

_____ _____   _____ _____
Seller or Buyer   Date   Real Estate Broker or Salesperson Date

_____ _____   _____
Seller or Buyer   Date   Brokerage Name

Ohio Revised Code Sections

4735.51 Agency Relationship - Disclosure Definitions

As used in sections 4735.51 to 4735.74 of the Revised Code:

(A) **"Agency" and "Agency relationship" mean a relationship in which a licensee represents another person in a real estate transaction.**

(B) **"Agency agreement" means a contract between a licensee and a client in which the client promises to pay the broker a valuable consideration, or agrees that the licensee may receive a valuable consideration from another, for performing an act that requires a real estate license under this chapter.**

(C) "Agent" and "real estate agent" mean a person licensed by this chapter to represent another in a real estate transaction.

(D) "Affiliated licensee" means a real estate broker or a real estate salesperson licensed by this chapter who is affiliated with a brokerage.

(E) "Brokerage" means a corporation, partnership, limited partnership, association, limited liability company, limited liability partnership, or sole proprietorship issued a broker's license. "Brokerage" includes the affiliated licensees who have been assigned management duties that include supervision of licensees whose duties may conflict with those of other affiliated licensees.

(F) **"Client" means a person who has entered into an agency relationship with a licensee.**

(G) **"Confidential information" means all information that a client directs to be kept confidential or that if disclosed would have an adverse effect on the client's position in the real estate transaction, except to the extent the agent is required by law to disclose such information, and all information that is required by law to be kept confidential.**

(H) **"Dual agency relationship" means any of the dual agency relationships set forth in section 4735.70 of the Revised Code.**

(I) "In-company transaction" means a real estate transaction in which the purchaser and seller are both represented by the same brokerage.

(J) "Licensee" means any individual licensed as a real estate broker or salesperson by the Ohio real estate commission pursuant to this chapter.

(K) **"Management level licensee" means a licensee who is employed by or affiliated with a real estate broker and who has supervisory responsibility over other licensees employed by or affiliated with that real estate broker.**

(L) **"Purchaser" means a party in a real estate transaction who is the potential transferee of property. "Purchaser" includes a person seeking to buy property and a person seeking to rent property as a tenant or lessee.**

(M) "Real estate transaction" means any act that is described in division (A) of section 4735.01 of the Revised Code or that is related to the execution of an act described in that section.

(N) **"Subagency" and "subagency relationship" mean an agency relationship in which a licensee acts for another licensee in performing duties for the client of that licensee.**

(O) **"Timely" means as soon as possible under the particular circumstances.**

4735.52 Scope of Chapter

The types of agency relationships permitted in a real estate transaction are determined by the provisions of this chapter. Except to the extent the duties of a real estate agent are specifically set forth in this chapter, or are otherwise modified by agreement, the duties of a real estate agent are determined by the common law.

4735.53 Agency Relationships Permitted

(A) The types of agency relationships a licensee may establish in a real estate transaction are limited to the following:

(1) An agency relationship between the licensee and the seller;

(2) An agency relationship between the licensee and the purchaser;

(3) A dual agency relationship between the licensee and both the seller and the purchaser;

(4) A subagency relationship between the licensee and the client of another licensee.

(B) **When an agency relationship is formed between a licensee and a client, all of the following also are considered the agent of that client:**

(1) The brokerage with whom the licensee is affiliated and, except as provided in division (C) of section 4735.70 of the Revised Code, the management level licensees in that brokerage who have direct supervisory duties over licensees ;

(2) Any licensee employed by, or affiliated with, the brokerage who receives confidential information from the agent of the client ;

(3) Any other licensee in the brokerage who assisted in establishing the agency relationship;

(4) Any licensee in the brokerage who specifically is appointed with the client's consent to represent that client.

(C) Except as otherwise provided in divisions (B)(1) to (4) of this section, another licensee who is affiliated with the same brokerage as the licensee is not an agent of that client .

(D) A payment or the promise of a payment to a licensee does not determine whether an agency relationship has been created between a licensee and a client or between other licensees in the brokerage with which the licensee is affiliated and that client.

4735.54 Written Company Policy for Types of Agency Relationships for Brokerage

Each brokerage shall develop and maintain a written company policy that sets forth the types of agency relationships that members of that brokerage may establish. The policy shall include provisions on whether any dual agency relationships set forth in section 4735.70 of the Revised Code are permitted. The policy shall also set forth procedures to ensure the protection of confidential information, and to ensure that the confidentiality provision extends to affiliated licensees of the brokerage. The policy developed and maintained under this section shall comply with the minimum standards established by rule by the Superintendent of real estate with the approval of the Ohio real estate commission. The development and maintenance of a policy under this section shall not relieve a brokerage from liability for the failure of the brokerage, any licensee of the brokerage, or any employee of the brokerage, to maintain the confidentiality of confidential information of a client. The brokerage shall provide a copy of its policy developed and maintained under this section to each client or prospective client upon request.

4735.55 Written Agency Agreements

(A) Each written agency agreement shall contain all of the following:

(1) An expiration date;

(2) A statement that it is illegal, pursuant to the Ohio fair housing law, division (H) of section 4112.02 of the Revised Code, and the federal fair housing law, 42 U.S.C.A. 3601, to refuse to sell, transfer, assign, rent, lease, sublease, or finance housing accommodations, refuse to negotiate for the sale or rental of housing accommodations, or otherwise deny or make unavailable housing accommodations because of race, color, religion, sex, familial status as defined in section 4112.01 of the Revised Code, ancestry, military status as defined in that section, disability as defined in that section, or national origin or to so discriminate in advertising the sale or rental of housing, in the financing of housing, or in the provision of real estate brokerage services;

(3) A statement defining the practice known as "blockbusting" and stating that it is illegal;

(4) A copy of the United States department of housing and urban development equal housing opportunity logotype, as set forth in 24 C.F.R. 109.30.

(B) Each written agency agreement shall contain a place for the licensee and the client to sign and date the agreement.

(C) A licensee shall furnish a copy of any written agency agreement to a client in a timely manner after the licensee and the client have signed and dated it.

4735.56 Written Brokerage Policy on Agency Required - Disclosure to Client

(A) Each brokerage shall develop a written brokerage policy on agency to be given to prospective sellers and purchasers in accordance with divisions (C) and (D) of this section.

(B) The brokerage policy on agency described in division (A) of this section shall include all of the following information:

(1) An explanation of the permissible agency relationships available under section 4735.53 of the Revised Code and the duties that the agent owes the agent's client;

(2) The brokerage's policy on representation of purchasers or sellers;

(3) Whether at some time during the agency relationship the brokerage and its licensee may act as a dual agent, and the options and consequences for the client if a dual agency situation arises including the right of the client to terminate the agency relationship and seek representation from another source;

(4) Whether at some time during the agency relationship, another licensee affiliated with the same brokerage as the licensee may become the exclusive agent for the other party in the transaction and whether each licensee will represent only the interests of that licensee's client;

(5) The brokerage's policy on cooperation with other brokerages, including whether the brokerage offers compensation to other brokerages or will seek compensation from other brokerages;

(6) That a brokerage that has a purchaser as a client represents the purchaser's interests even though the seller's agent or the seller may compensate that purchaser's brokerage;

(7) That the signature of the purchaser or the seller indicates acknowledgement of receipt of the brokerage policy on agency.

(C) A licensee acting as a seller's agent shall provide the seller with the brokerage policy on agency described in this section prior to marketing or showing the seller's real estate and shall obtain a signature from the seller acknowledging receipt unless the seller refuses to provide a signature. If the seller refuses to provide a signature, the licensee shall note this on the policy.

(D) A licensee working directly with a purchaser in a real estate transaction, whether as the purchaser's agent, the seller's agent, or the seller's subagent, shall provide the purchaser with the brokerage policy on agency described in this section and obtain a signature from the purchaser acknowledging receipt of the policy unless the purchaser refuses to provide a signature. If the purchaser refuses to provide a signature, the licensee shall note this on the policy. Except as provided in division (E) of this section, the licensee shall provide the brokerage policy on agency to a purchaser prior to the earliest of the following actions of the licensee:

(1) Initiating a prequalification evaluation to determine whether the purchaser has the financial ability to purchase or lease a particular real estate property;

(2) Requesting specific financial information from the purchaser to determine the purchaser's ability to purchase or finance real estate in a particular price range;

(3) Showing the real estate to the purchaser other than at an open house;

(4) Discussing, with the purchaser, the making of an offer to purchase or lease real estate;

(5) Submitting an offer to purchase or lease real estate on behalf of the purchaser.

(E) If the earliest event described in division (D) of this section is by telephone or electronic mail, the licensee shall disclose by that same medium the nature of the agency relationship that the licensee has with both the seller and the purchaser. The licensee shall provide the purchaser with the brokerage policy on agency described in this section at the first meeting with the purchaser following this disclosure of the agency relationship.

(F) A licensee acting as a seller's agent is not required to provide a purchaser with the brokerage policy on agency described in this section except in the case of an event described in division (D) of this section.

(G) The requirements of this section regarding provision of a brokerage policy on agency do not apply in any of the following situations:

(1) The rental or leasing of residential premises as defined in section 5321.01 of the Revised Code, if the rental or lease agreement can be performed in eighteen months or less;

(2) The referral of a prospective purchaser or seller to another licensee;

(3) Transactions involving the sale, lease, or exchange of foreign real estate as defined in division (E) of section 4735.01 of the Revised Code;

(4) Transactions involving the sale of a cemetery lot or a cemetery interment right.

4735.57 Agency Disclosure Statement - Dual Agency Disclosure

(A) The Superintendent of real estate, with the approval of the Ohio real estate commission, shall establish by rule an agency disclosure statement. The agency disclosure statement shall contain a place for the licensee and the parties to the transaction to sign and date the statement and shall contain sections for the disclosure or explanation of all of the following:

(1) Unless confidential, the names of all the parties in the transaction;

(2) The address of the real estate being sold or leased;

(3) The name of the licensee or licensees and the brokerage with which each licensee is affiliated;

(4) The party that each licensee in the named brokerage represents in the transaction;

(5) If a licensee representing a purchaser of real estate and a licensee representing the seller of that real estate are affiliated with the same brokerage, whether the two licensees are acting as dual agents or are individually representing the purchaser and seller separately;

(6) If only one licensee is involved in the transaction, whether that licensee is a dual agent or represents only one party to the transaction;

(7) If both the purchaser and the seller are represented by licensees affiliated with the same brokerage, that the brokerage is a dual agent;

(8) That the signature of the client indicates the client's informed consent to the agency relationship and that if the client does not understand the agency disclosure statement, the client should consult an attorney.

(B) The agency disclosure statement shall specify the duties of a licensee acting as a dual agent and shall contain sections disclosing all of the following:

(1) An explanation of the nature of a dual agency relationship, including a statement that in serving as a dual agent, licensees in the brokerage represent two clients whose interests are, or at times could be, different or adverse;

(2) That as a result of the dual agency relationship, the dual agent may not be able to advocate on behalf of the client to the same extent the agent may have if the agent represented only one client;

(3) A description of the duties the brokerage and its affiliated licensees and employees owe to each client, including the duty of confidentiality;

(4) That neither the brokerage nor its affiliated licensees have any material relationship with either client other than incidental to the transaction, or if the brokerage or its affiliated licensees have a material relationship, a disclosure of the nature of the relationship. For purposes of this division, "material relationship" means any actually known personal, familial, or business relationship between the brokerage or an affiliated licensee and a client that could impair the ability of the brokerage or affiliated licensee to exercise lawful and independent judgment relative to another client.

(5) That as a dual agent, the brokerage cannot engage in conduct that is contrary to the interests or instructions of one party or act in a biased manner on behalf of one party;

(6) A section specifying the source of compensation to the real estate broker;

(7) That the client does not have to consent to the dual agency relationship, and the options available to the client for representation in the transaction

if the client does not consent, including the right of the client to terminate the agency relationship and seek representation from another source;

(8) That the consent to the dual agency relationship by the client has been given voluntarily, that the signature indicates informed consent, and that the duties of a licensee acting as a dual agent disclosed to the client pursuant to division (B) of this section have been read and understood.

4735.58 When Disclosure Statements to be Provided

(A) A licensee who is a purchaser's agent or a seller's subagent working with a purchaser shall present the agency disclosure statement described in section 4735.57 of the Revised Code to the purchaser and request the purchaser to sign and date the statement no later than the preparation of an offer to purchase or lease, or a written request for a proposal to lease. The licensee shall deliver the statement signed by the purchaser to the seller's agent, or to the seller if the seller is not represented by an agent. Prior to presenting the seller with either a written offer to purchase or lease, or a written request for a proposal to lease, the seller's agent, or the purchaser's agent if the seller is not represented by an agent, shall present the agency disclosure statement to the seller and request the seller to sign and date the statement.

(B) A licensee selling property at auction shall, prior to the auction, verbally disclose to the audience that the licensee represents the seller in the real estate transaction. The licensee shall provide the agency disclosure statement described in section 4735.57 of the Revised Code to the successful bidder prior to the bidder's signing a purchase contract.

(C) Evidence that a licensee has failed to comply with this section constitutes prima-facie evidence of misconduct in violation of division (A)(6) of section 4735.18 of the Revised Code.

(D) The disclosure requirements of this section do not apply in any of the following situations:

(1) The rental or leasing of residential premises as defined in section 5321.01 of the Revised Code, if the rental or lease agreement can be performed in eighteen months or less;

(2) The referral of a prospective purchaser or seller to another licensee;

(3) Transactions involving the sale, lease, or exchange of foreign real estate as defined in division (E) of section 4735.01 of the Revised Code;

(4) Transactions involving the sale of a cemetery lot or a cemetery interment right.

(E) The licensee is obligated to perform all duties imposed on a real estate agent at common law except to the extent the duties are inconsistent with the duties prescribed in this chapter or are otherwise modified by agreement.

4735.59 Changing the Party a Licensee Represents

To change the party a licensee represents in a real estate transaction after an agency disclosure statement has been signed and dated or following verbal disclosure of the agency relationship, the licensee shall obtain written consent from the party originally represented to represent another party in the transaction. The licensee shall promptly notify all persons who had been notified of the original relationship.

4735.60 Licensee Representing Purchaser Disclosures

A licensee representing a purchaser shall do the following:

(A) Disclose to the licensee representing the seller, or if the seller is not represented, disclose to the seller, that the licensee represents the purchaser in the transaction. This disclosure shall take place during the first contact the licensee has with any employee or licensee of the brokerage with which the seller's agent is affiliated, or if the seller is not represented by a licensee, during the first contact with the seller.

(B) If the seller is not represented by a licensee, verbally disclose during the first contact with the seller, any intention of seeking compensation from the seller.

4735.61 Prohibiting False Information

No licensee shall knowingly give false information to any party in a real estate transaction.

4735.62 Fiduciary Duties Generally

In representing any client in an agency or subagency relationship, the licensee shall be a fiduciary of the client and shall use the licensee's best efforts to further the interest of the client including, but not limited to, doing all of the following:

(A) Exercising reasonable skill and care in representing the client and carrying out the responsibilities of the agency relationship;

(B) Performing the terms of any written agency agreement;

(C) Following any lawful instructions of the client;

(D) Performing all duties specified in this chapter in a manner that is loyal to the interest of the client;

(E) Complying with all requirements of this chapter and other applicable statutes, rules, and regulations, including the Ohio fair housing law, division (H) of section 4112.02 of the Revised Code, and the federal fair housing law, 42 U.S.C.A. 3601 ;

(F) Disclosing to the client any material facts of the transaction of which the licensee is aware or should be aware in the exercise of reasonable skill and care and that are not confidential information pursuant to a current or prior agency or dual agency relationship;

(G) Advising the client to obtain expert advice related to material matters when necessary or appropriate;

(H) Accounting in a timely manner for all moneys and property received in which the client has or may have an interest;

(I) Keeping confidential all confidential information, unless the licensee is permitted to disclose the information pursuant to division (B) of section 4735.74 of the Revised Code. This requirement includes not disclosing confidential information to any licensee who is not an agent of the client.

4735.621 Waiver of Fiduciary Duties

(A) The duties required of a licensee under section 4735.62 of the Revised Code may not be waived by a client.

(B) A licensee shall perform the duties required under section 4735.63 or 4735.65 of the Revised Code unless the client agrees to waive these duties, and signs a waiver of duties statement pursuant to division (C) of this section.

(C) The Superintendent of real estate, with the approval of the Ohio real estate commission, shall establish by rule a waiver of duties statement that shall contain the following:

(1) The fiduciary duties required of all licensees under section 4735.62 of the Revised Code;

(2) A list of those duties contained in section 4735.63 or 4735.65 of the Revised Code, which shall be set forth in a manner that allows for the parties to indicate which of those duties are being waived;

(3) A statement that no other licensee is required to perform the waived duty on behalf of the client;

(4) A statement that legal counsel or other professionals may be hired by the client;

(5) A place for the client and licensee to sign and date the statement.

4735.63 Representing Seller in Agency Relationship - Duty to Promote Interests of Client

(A) In representing a seller in an agency relationship, a licensee shall :

(1) Seek a purchase offer at a price and with terms acceptable to the seller. Unless the seller so directs, the licensee is not obligated to seek additional offers if the property is subject to a contract of sale, lease, or letter of intent to lease;

(2) Accept delivery of and present any purchase offer to the seller in a timely manner, even if the property is subject to a contract of sale, lease, or letter of intent to lease;

(3) Within the scope of knowledge required for licensure, answer the seller's questions and provide information to the seller regarding any offers or counteroffers;

(4) Assist the seller in developing, communicating, and presenting offers or counteroffers;

(5) Within the scope of knowledge required for licensure, answer the seller's questions regarding the steps the seller must take to fulfill the terms of any contract.

(B) A licensee does not breach any duty or obligation to a seller with whom the licensee has an agency relationship by showing alternative properties to a prospective purchaser or by acting as an agent or subagent for other sellers.

(C) Nothing in this section shall be construed as permitting a licensee to perform any act or service that constitutes the practice of law.

4735.64 Representing Seller in Agency Relationship - Prohibited Acts

In representing a seller in an agency relationship, no licensee shall do either of the following without the knowledge and consent of the seller:

(A) Extend an offer of subagency to other licensees;

(B) Offer compensation to a broker who represents a purchaser.

4735.65 Representing Buyer in Agency Relationship - Duty to Promote Interests of Client

(A) In representing a purchaser in an agency relationship, a licensee shall:

(1) Seek a property at a price and with purchase or lease terms acceptable to the purchaser. Unless the client so directs, the licensee is not obligated to seek additional purchase or lease possibilities if the purchaser is a party to a contract to purchase property, or has entered into a lease or has extended a letter of intent to lease.

(2) Within the scope of knowledge required for licensure, answer the purchaser's questions and provide information to the purchaser regarding any offers or counteroffers;

(3) Assist the purchaser in developing, communicating, and presenting offers or counteroffers;

(4) Present any offer to purchase or lease to the seller or the seller's agent in a timely manner, even if the property is subject to a contract of sale, lease, or letter of intent to lease, and accept delivery of and present any counteroffers to the purchaser in a timely manner;

(5) Within the scope of knowledge required for licensure, answer the purchaser's questions regarding the steps the purchaser must take to fulfill the terms of any contract.

(B) A licensee does not breach any duty or obligation to the purchaser by showing the same properties to other purchasers or by acting as an agent or subagent for other purchasers, or as an agent or subagent for sellers, except that any dual agency relationship must be disclosed to a client pursuant to section 4735.71 of the Revised Code.

(C) Nothing in this section shall be construed as permitting a licensee to perform any act or service that constitutes the practice of law.

4735.66 Representing Buyer in Agency Relationship - Prohibited Acts

In representing a purchaser in an agency relationship, no licensee shall do either of the following without the knowledge and consent of the purchaser:

(A) Extend an offer of subagency to other licensees;

(B) Accept compensation from a broker who represents a seller.

4735.67 Disclosures to Purchaser

(A) A licensee shall disclose to any purchaser all material facts of which the licensee has actual knowledge pertaining to the physical condition of the property that the purchaser would not discover by a reasonably diligent inspection, including material defects in the property, environmental contamination, and information that any statute or rule requires be disclosed. For purposes of this division, actual knowledge of such material facts shall be inferred to the licensee if the licensee acts with reckless disregard for the truth.

(B) A licensee is not required to discover latent defects in the property or to advise on matters outside of the scope of the knowledge required for real estate licensure, or to verify the accuracy or completeness of statements made by the seller, unless the licensee is aware of information that should reasonably cause the licensee to question the accuracy or completeness of such statements.

(C) Nothing in this section limits any obligation of a seller to disclose to a purchaser all material facts known by the seller pertaining to the physical condition of the property, nor does it limit the obligation of the prospective purchaser to inspect the physical condition of the property.

(D) Nothing in this section limits any obligation of a purchaser to disclose to a seller all material adverse facts known by the purchaser pertaining to the purchaser's financial ability to perform the terms of the transaction.

(E) No cause of action shall arise on behalf of any person against a licensee for disclosing information in compliance with this section, unless the information is materially inaccurate and the disclosure by the licensee was made in bad faith or was made with reckless disregard for the truth.

4735.68 Liability for False Information

(A) A licensee is not liable to any party for false information that the licensee's client provided to the licensee and that the licensee in turn provided to another party in the real estate transaction, unless the licensee had actual knowledge that the information was false or acted with reckless disregard for the truth.

(B) No cause of action shall arise on behalf of any person against a client for any misrepresentation a licensee made while representing that client unless the client had actual knowledge of the licensee's misrepresentation.

4735.69 Assisting Party Who is Not a Client

(A) A licensee may assist a party who is not the licensee's client in a real estate transaction by doing any of the following:

(1) Providing information regarding lenders, inspectors, attorneys, insurance agents, surveyors, draftspersons, architects, schools, shopping facilities, places of worship, and other similar information;

(2) Providing market information or other information obtained from a property listing service or public records.

(B) A licensee who assists a party who is not the licensee's client as permitted in division (A) of this section does not violate the agency relationship with the client, and provision of the services for that party neither forms nor implies any agency relationship with that party.

4735.70 Dual Agency Definitions

The following are dual agents under this chapter:

(A) A licensee who represents both the purchaser and the seller as clients in the same real estate transaction;

(B) A brokerage that represents both the purchaser and the seller as clients in the same real estate transaction;

(C) A management level licensee who represents a client in an in-company transaction. *If there* is more than one management level licensee affiliated with the brokerage and either of the following applies, the management level licensee is not a dual agent:

(1) The management level licensee personally represents either the seller or the purchaser in a transaction, in which case the management level licensee will represent only the interests of that licensee's client.

(2) The management level licensee is the purchaser or seller in a transaction and will represent only that licensee's interest.

4735.71 Dual Agency - Disclosure Statement

(A) No licensee or brokerage shall participate in a dual agency relationship described in section 4735.70 of the Revised Code unless both the seller and the purchaser in the transaction have full knowledge of the dual representation and consent in writing to the dual representation on the agency disclosure statement described in section 4735.57 of the Revised Code. Before a licensee obtains the consent of any party to a dual agency relationship, the licensee shall disclose to both the purchaser and the seller all relevant information necessary to enable each party to make an informed decision as to whether to consent to the dual agency relationship. If, after consent is obtained, there is a material change in the information disclosed to the purchaser and the seller, the licensee shall disclose the change of information to the purchaser and the seller and give them an opportunity to revoke their consent.

(B) No brokerage shall participate in a dual agency relationship described in division (C) of section 4735.70 of the Revised Code, unless each of the following conditions is met:

(1) The brokerage has established a procedure under section 4735.54 of the Revised Code under which licensees, including management level licensees, who represent one client will not have access to and will not obtain confidential information concerning another client of the brokerage involved in the dual agency transaction.

(2) *Each* licensee fulfills the licensee's duties exclusively to *the licensee's* client.

4735.72 Dual Agency - Brokerage and Management Level Licensees

(A) The brokerage and management level licensees in a brokerage in which there is a dual agency relationship described in section 4735.70 of the Revised Code shall do each of the following:

(1) Objectively supervise the affiliated licensees in the fulfillment of their duties and obligations to their respective clients;

(2) Refrain from advocating or negotiating on behalf of either the seller or the purchaser;

(3) Refrain from disclosing to any other employee of the brokerage or any party or client, any confidential information of a client of which the brokerage or management level licensee becomes aware and from utilizing or allowing to be utilized for the benefit of another client, any confidential information obtained from a client.

(B) When two licensees affiliated with the same brokerage represent separate clients in the same transaction, each affiliated licensee shall do both of the following:

(1) Serve as the agent of only the party in the transaction the licensee agreed to represent;

(2) Fulfill the duties owed to the respective client as set forth in this chapter and as agreed in the agency agreement.

(C)(1) In all cases, a management level licensee shall keep information of the client or brokerage confidential.

(2) Nothing in this section prohibits the brokerage or management level licensees in the brokerage from providing factual, nonconfidential information that presents or suggests objective options or solutions, or assisting the parties in an unbiased manner to negotiate or fulfill the terms of the purchase contract or lease, provided that confidential information of a client is not utilized in any manner in formulating such suggestions or providing this assistance.

(D) No cause of action shall arise on behalf of any person against a licensee in a dual agency relationship for making disclosures to the parties that are permitted or required by this chapter or that have been made on the agency disclosure statement. Making permitted disclosures does not terminate any agency relationship between a licensee and a client.

(E)(1) If a brokerage determines that confidential information of one client in a dual agency relationship has become known to any licensee employed by or affiliated with the brokerage who is representing the other client in the dual agency relationship, as a result of the failure of the brokerage, its licensees, or its employees to maintain such confidentiality, the brokerage shall do both of the following:

(a) Notify both clients of the fact immediately in writing;

(b) Offer to resign representation of both clients.

(2) If either client elects to accept the resignation, the brokerage shall not be entitled to any compensation from that client. If either client does not accept the resignation, the brokerage may continue to represent that client.

(3) A licensee who obtains confidential information concerning another client of the brokerage in a dual agency relationship shall not, under any circumstances, disclose that information to or use that information for the benefit of the licensee's client.

(F) A client of a brokerage who is involved in a dual agency relationship may bring an individual action against a brokerage and any licensee who has failed to comply with the procedure described in division (B)(1) of section 4735.71 of the Revised Code to recover actual damages and to rescind an agency agreement with the brokerage.

4735.74 Duties Following Closing of Transaction

Unless otherwise agreed in writing, a licensee owes no further duty to a client after performance of all duties or after any contract has terminated or expired, except for both of the following:

(A) Providing the client with an accounting of all moneys and property relating to the transaction;

(B) Keeping confidential all information received during the course of the transaction unless;

(1) The client permits disclosure;

(2) Disclosure is required by law or by court order;

(3) The information becomes public from a source other than the licensee;

(4) The information is necessary to prevent a crime the client intends to commit;

(5) Disclosure is necessary to defend the brokerage or its licensees against an accusation of wrongful conduct or to establish or defend a claim that a commission is owed on a transaction.

Ohio Administrative Code Section

1301:5-6-01 Management Level Licensee

(A) A licensee will be found to be a management level licensee under division (K) of section 4735.51 of the Revised Code if both of the following apply:

 (1) The licensee has been assigned management duties that involve oversight responsibilities for the brokerage's main office, a branch office, or a division within that brokerage; and,

 (2) Those management duties include the supervision of affiliated licensees whose agency duties to their clients may conflict with those of other licensees affiliated with the brokerage.

(B) Unless a licensee meets the requirements of paragraph (A) of this rule, the following are not considered to be management level licensees:

 (1) Any licensee who has an ownership interest in the brokerage with which the licensee is affiliated, unless acting in a manner that is calculated to influence or have an effect on a real estate transaction, other than a transaction in which the licensee is a direct participant.

 (2) Any licensee who is an officer of the brokerage with which the licensee is affiliated, unless acting in a manner that is calculated to influence or have an effect on a real estate transaction, other than a transaction in which the licensee is a direct participant.

 (3) A licensee who voluntarily provides advice and/or assistance to other licensees affiliated with the brokerage but who does not do so as an assigned duty, unless compensated for such advice and/or assistance.

(C) Supervision shall include, but, not be limited to, the general oversight of, or the direction of, activities conducted by other real estate licensees affiliated with the brokerage.

(D) The assignment of supervisory duties to management level licensees does not relieve the brokerage and its brokers from their responsibility to actively oversee and direct the operations of the business conducted on behalf of the brokerage.

1301:5-6-02 Open Houses and Referrals

(A) A licensee who acts as a host at an open house on behalf of a listing agent will only be considered to be the agent of the seller if one of the following applies:

 (1) The licensee was appointed by the listing agent or the brokerage to represent the seller and the seller agreed in writing to that representation;

 (2) The licensee assisted in establishing the agency relationship;

 (3) The licensee received confidential information from the listing agent; or,

 (4) The licensee is a management level licensee as defined in division (K) of section 4735.51 of the Revised Code, except as provided in division (C) of section 4735.70 of the Revised Code.

(B) The licensee will not be found to have assisted in establishing an agency relationship as provided in section 4735.53 of the Revised Code as a result of referring a prospective purchaser or seller to another licensee or receiving a referral fee. However, if the licensee making the referral, participates in the real estate transaction which results from the referral and receives a referral fee, the payment of that referral fee must be disclosed to all parties to the transaction. For purposes of this rule, the terms "referral" and "referring" have the same meaning as contained in paragraph (C) of rule 1301:5-5-06 of the Administrative Code.

1301:5-6-03 Mandatory Company Policy

The written company policy required under section 4735.54 of the Revised Code shall, at a minimum, address the following information and be applicable to all offices of the brokerage:

(A) The types of agency relationships the affiliated licensees of the brokerage may establish including an explanation of each agency relationship authorized and whether any dual agency relationships are permitted;

(B) A current list of positions in the brokerage, if any, which are designated by the brokerage as management level;

(C) The procedure to be followed for an affiliated licensee to be appointed to represent the client of another affiliated licensee, including the procedure for giving prior notification and obtaining approval of the client for this representation;

(D) The type of agency relationship that shall be established and the disclosures that shall be made when licensees are handling real estate transactions involving persons with whom they have a personal, business, or familial relationship;

(E) The type of agency relationship that shall be established and the disclosures that shall be made when licensees are handling real estate transactions involving themselves or any affiliated licensee as a party to the transaction;

(F) The procedures to be followed to ensure that confidential information is not disclosed in violation of the licensee's agency duties. These procedures shall include those steps affiliated licensees are required to follow to protect confidential information from being disclosed to other licensees within the brokerage who are not bound by the agency relationship. This policy must address the following:

(1) Office files;

(2) Computerized records and messages;

(3) Office meetings and discussions;

(4) Facsimile transmissions;

(5) Telephone messages, inter-office messages, and any kind of conversations;

(6) Meetings and conversations with clients.

(G) If the brokerage practices dual agency, the procedures to be followed by a licensee in the event any of the following occurs:

(1) A party to a real estate transaction refuses to consent to dual agency;

(2) A party to a real estate transaction seeks to terminate an agency relationship as the result of an attempt to create a dual agency relationship;

(3) There is a material change to any of the information that was previously disclosed to any party prior to obtaining full consent to the dual agency.

(H) The procedures to be followed by a licensee who wishes to change an agency relationship, to include but not be limited to procedures for securing the written consent of the client(s) to such change; and,

(I) The types of cooperation, and explanation thereof, which are offered other brokerages, including:

(1) Whether the brokerage offers subagency;

(2) Whether the brokerage offers compensation to subagencies and buyer's brokerages;

(3) Whether the brokerage accepts compensation from other brokerages; and,

(4) Whether the types of cooperation are offered on a consistent and equal basis to all brokerages.

1301:5-6-04 Agency Agreements

(A) Divisions (A)(2) to (A)(4) of section 4735.55 of the Revised Code shall only apply to an agency agreement in which the property identified on the agency agreement falls within the definition of housing accommodation as contained in any municipal, state, or federal fair housing laws and regulations and the disclosures required pursuant to section 4735.56 of the Revised Code.

(B) Unless exempt under paragraph (A) of this rule, the statement regarding blockbusting shall read as follows:

"It is also illegal, for profit, to induce or attempt to induce a person to sell or rent a dwelling by representations regarding the entry into the neighborhood of a person or persons belonging to one of the protected classes."

1301:5-6-05 Consumer Guide to Agency Relationships

(A) A broker shall develop a consumer guide to agency relationships that contains the written disclosures required by division (B) of section 4735.56 of the Revised Code.

(B) The consumer guide to agency relationships shall:

(1) Be entitled "Consumer Guide to Agency Relationships". The title font size shall be no less than fourteen points;

(2) Contain the brokerage name and fair housing logo. The brokerage may also include the brokerage logo, a brokerage franchise name or insignia indicating membership in a real estate organization. The name of any salesperson, team advertising name, unlicensed person or entity shall not be included;

(3) Contain the disclosures required pursuant to divisions (A)(2) and (A)(3) of section 4735.55 of the Revised Code, for housing accommodation and vacant land transactions only, in a font size of no less than nine points;

(4) Contain a disclosure that Ohio law requires the guide to be provided to prospective sellers, lessors, purchasers, lessees and the agent is required to obtain their signature acknowledging receipt of the guide;

(5) Contain a disclosure of the brokerage policy on customers that are unrepresented;

(6) Provide all required disclosures in a font size of no less than eleven points;

(7) Contain a description of only those forms of agency permissible pursuant to section 4735.53 of the Revised Code.

(C) Other licensees within the same brokerage who later perform acts described in division (C) or (D) of section 4735.56 of the Revised Code are not required to make the disclosures described in section 4735.56 of the Revised Code if previously provided by another licensee within the same brokerage.

(D) The acknowledgement required pursuant to divisions (C) and (D) of section 4735.56 of the Revised Code may be on a document separate from the "Consumer Guide to Agency Relationships". The acknowledgement shall not be contained within any contract, agreement or addendum to which the buyer or seller is a party.

1301:5-6-06 Agency Disclosure

(A) (1) If a purchaser or seller declines to acknowledge receipt of the "Consumer Guide to Agency Relationships" required pursuant to section 4735.56 of the Revised Code or sign an agency disclosure form that is presented as required by section 4735.58 of the Revised Code, the licensee shall note the following on the bottom of the form:

(a) The party(ies) to whom the form was presented;

(b) The date and time the form was presented;

(c) The fact that the party(ies) declines to sign the form; and,

(d) The reason the party(ies) declines to sign the form if known.

(2) If a purchaser or seller declines to acknowledge receipt of "Consumer Guide to Agency Relationships" or sign an agency disclosure statement that is presented as required by section 4735.58 of the Revised Code, notice thereof shall immediately be communicated to a management level licensee in the brokerage who supervises the licensee.

(3) The brokerage shall, for a period of three years from the date of the transaction, maintain a copy of the form containing the information required by paragraph (B)(1) of this rule.

(B) No licensee shall fail to deliver or present an offer to purchase or lease because a party has declined to sign an agency disclosure statement or because an agency disclosure statement was not received.

(C) No modification, alteration, addition, deletion, or reduction in size of the agency disclosure statement shall be permitted. This provision shall not be construed as prohibiting compliance with the requirements of the Americans with Disabilities Act.

1301:5-6-07 Agency Disclosure Statement

See pages 69 - 70 of this textbook for the form used for the agency disclosure statement, as required by section 4735.57 of the Revised Code.

1301:5-6-08 Appointment of Licensees

(A) When an agency relationship is formed between a licensee and client, that client may delegate to that licensee, the authority to specifically appoint other licensees within the same brokerage to represent the client's interests. This delegation must be done in writing and must be signed by the client. It must also include language notifying the client he has the right to veto the appointment of any other licensee within the brokerage.

(B) If any delegation of authority to appoint as outlined in paragraph (A) of this rule is made, the licensee must notify the client, at the time the appointment takes place, that such an appointment is being made.

1301:5-6-09 Negotiations with a Purchaser or Tenant

(A) Except as provided in section 4735.75 of the Revised Code, a licensee shall not negotiate the sale, exchange or lease of any real property directly with the purchaser or tenant if the licensee has actual knowledge that the purchaser or tenant has entered into a written outstanding agency agreement that grants exclusive agency to another real estate broker.

(B) A licensee is not required to ask a purchaser or tenant whether they have entered into such a written, exclusive agency relationship with another broker; except that a licensee is required to inquire as to the nature of a purchaser or tenant's relationship with another licensee if he has reasonable cause to believe the purchaser or tenant may be currently represented by another licensee.

(C) A licensee may rely upon a definitive representation by a purchaser or tenant that they are not currently subject to a written exclusive agency agreement with another broker and is not required to verify the accuracy of such a representation by a purchaser or tenant. Following such a representation by a purchaser or tenant a licensee may enter into direct negotiations with a purchaser or tenant.

(D) If the purchaser or tenant does not know whether they have entered into a written exclusive agency agreement with another licensee, a licensee is not permitted ot to negotiate with that purchaser or tenant until the purchaser or tenant can verify that they have not entered into such a written exclusive agreement with another licensee.

True/False Questions

____ 1. Ohio Agency law assumes all licensees represent the seller.

____ 2. Agency disclosure must be made to the seller at the time a listing is signed.

____ 3. When involved in a dual agency, a licensee must disclose if the buyer is his mother.

____ 4. Agency law is the same in Ohio for residential and commercial real estate.

____ 5. There is one Agency Disclosure Statement form for all disclosure situations.

____ 6. Ohio law does not require an agency disclosure to be made to all guests at an open house.

____ 7. Ohio law no longer permits subagency with other firms.

____ 8. A licensee may not represent both the buyer and seller in the same transaction.

____ 9. The Ohio Agency Disclosure Statement must include Fair Housing language.

____ 10. All companies must permit designated agency.

____ 11. All companies must have a written agency policy.

____ 12. The full, written company policy must be given to each buyer and seller.

____ 13. Every one who plans to bid at a real estate auction must be given a written disclosure.

____ 14. A dual agent may disclose confidential information with the written permission of the client.

____ 15. Management-level licensees have different agency responsibilities from the average licensee.

Multiple Choice Questions

1. Harold, a licensee, made a listing presentation on June 14. The sellers sign a listing agreement on June 15 with a stipulation that the for sale sign not be erected nor showings scheduled until July 1. Harold agrees and puts up the sign when the office goes on tour July 2. When must the Consumer Guide to Agency Relationship form be given to the seller?
   a. June 14
   b. June 15
   c. July 1
   d. July 2

2. Maude takes a listing on a property. If Maude and her broker represent the seller but the other agents in the company do not, what type of agency does Maude's company practice?
   a. seller agency
   b. subagency
   c. split agency
   d. dual agency

3. Ralph meets the Jones's at an open house on October 15. He goes to the home to qualify them on October 17 and shows them property on October 19. If Ralph writes an offer for the Jones on October 20, on what date should he have made the agency disclosure?
   a. October 15
   b. October 17
   c. October 19
   d. October 20

4. Larry represents a purchaser. Larry is a
   a. seller's agent.
   b. buyer's agent.
   c. split agent.
   d. dual agent.

5. You are acting as a disclosed dual agent. Which of the following would be a violation?
   a. treating both clients honestly
   b. disclosing latent defects in the property
   c. writing the offer as dictated by the parties
   d. disclosing that the buyer went bankrupt one year ago

Quiz Answers

True/False		Multiple Choice	
1.	F	1.	D
2.	F	2.	C
3.	T	3.	D
4.	T	4.	B
5.	T	5.	D
6.	T		
7.	F		
8.	F		
9.	T		
10.	F		
11.	T		
12.	F		
13.	F		
14.	T		
15.	T		

Common Real Estate Forms

Residential Property Disclosure Form

Environmental Concerns With Real Estate

There are four specific hazards listed on the Residential Property Disclosure Form:

1. Lead-Based Paint (covered in detail starting on page 96)
2. Asbestos: A fibrous material once very common in many building materials because of its insulating and heat-resistant value, but no longer used because it is believed to cause cancer.
3. Urea-Formaldehyde Foam Insulation: A type of blown-in insulation that has been banned in many parts of the U.S. because of the potential health risks from toxic fumes.
4. Radon Gas: A naturally occurring, odorless, colorless, radioactive gas that emanates from rocks and has been identified as a cancer-causing agent.

Residential Property Disclosure Form Analysis

Analysis by Ohio Division of Real Estate of the Residential Property Disclosure Form

1. Applies to the transfer of "residential real property" after July 1, 1993. Residential Real Property is defined as real property that is improved by a building or other structure that has 1 to 4 dwelling units.

    13 different exemptions to the disclosure requirement

2. Requirement is imposed upon the seller to complete the property disclosure form and provide it to each prospective transferee **AS SOON AS PRACTICABLE**.

    can be delivered by ordinary mail, certified mail, fax, or personal delivery

3. If information is unknown to the seller, a "good faith" approximation can be made.

4. Seller is not liable for any error, inaccuracy, or omission of any item of information required to be disclosed if the error, inaccuracy, or omission was in good faith and was not within seller's "actual knowledge", or was based on information provided by another (e.g., agent).

5. If information disclosed is subsequently rendered inaccurate after delivery of the disclosure form, there is no requirement that the seller update the information to the prospective buyer. The legislation only provides that the information **may be** amended "at any time" following delivery of the form.

6. This disclosure requirement shall not bar any legal or equitable defense that a seller may assert in a civil action commenced by a buyer (i.e., caveat emptor).

7. Subject to the rescission provision, the transfer of real property is not invalidated due to failure of transferor to provide to the transferee the disclosure form, unless transferor is otherwise obligated to disclose an item of information.

8. If the transferee receives a disclosure form or an amendment of the form after a contract is entered, the transferee may rescind the agreement without any legal liability. Upon rescission of the agreement the transferee is entitled to the return of, and the transferor shall return, any deposits.

    Rescission may occur only if the transferee's rescission is delivered to the transferor or his agent within three business days following the date the transferee receives the disclosure form or the amendment.

No right of rescission if any transferee receives a disclosure form or an amendment prior to submission of an offer and the transferor's acceptance of the offer.

9. If no disclosure form provided, transferee may rescind without liability, but must rescind by the earlier of 30 days after the offer is accepted or closing.

Issues/Areas of Concerns

1. Disclosure, for it to be meaningful to the buyer, should be at first meeting with seller or agent, or prior to submission and acceptance of the offer, whichever is earlier. (Not "as soon as practicable"—this could be after the contract is entered, which could be late.)

2. The agent, for licensing purposes, should be held responsible for the dissemination of information that the agent knows, or has reason to know, is false, misleading, or inaccurate.

3. If information is unknown to the transferor, or not within his actual knowledge, this fact should be stated. It would seem more in the public interest to have a seller make no representation when they have no actual knowledge. "Good Faith" approximation is too subject to challenge. Providing approximations also increases the likelihood that erroneous information will be provided. Further, if a buyer relies on a good faith approximation which proves to be inaccurate, there is no damage recovery by the buyer against the seller for the error or inaccuracy. In fairness to the buyer, if a representation is made, the seller (and/or agent) should be responsible for its accuracy, unless the seller or agent is relying on information provided by another, (i.e., seller gives inaccurate information obtained from the auditor's office as to the current taxes on the property.)

4. Transferor should be responsible for updating information on the disclosure if it is subsequently rendered inaccurate. The update should be as soon as practicable, but not later than the presentation and acceptance of the offer. (If offer is already accepted, as soon as practicable, but not later than the closing date.)

5. Delivery of disclosure form by ordinary mail is very susceptible to challenge as there is no verification of receipt. Could have a substantial impact in rescission provisions.

6. Legislation should clarify that if rescission pursuant to section (k)(2), the transferor "or his agent" shall return any deposits made (line 9.27).

7. If the right of rescission can be waived by the transferee, (line 10.14) the waiver should be required to be *in writing through a separate document*.

8. Who will be distributing and printing the form?

9. If the transferor can still raise the defense of *caveat emptor*, what's the statute attempting to accomplish? The statute does not provide additional protection to the seller. It does not assure that the buyer is provided with accurate information as the transferor is permitted to approximate/guess on matters which the transferor does not have actual knowledge without risk of liability. In addition, the buyer is still subject to the defense of *caveat emptor* if an observable (patent) defect is not disclosed. Further, while the statute attempts to shift liability away from the licensees, this does not appear to be accomplished as the licensee can still be sued for providing false or misleading information concerning a property.

2013

STATE OF OHIO DEPARTMENT
OF COMMERCE

RESIDENTIAL PROPERTY DISCLOSURE FORM

Pursuant to section 5302.30 of the Revised Code and rule 1301:5-6-10 of the Administrative Code.

TO BE COMPLETED BY OWNER (*Please Print*)

Property Address:

_____

Owners Name(s):

_____

Date: _____, 20_____

Owner ☐ is ☐ is not occupying the property. If owner is occupying the property, since what date: _____

If owner is not occupying the property, since what date: _____

THE FOLLOWING STATEMENTS OF THE OWNER ARE BASED ON OWNER'S ACTUAL KNOWLEDGE

A) WATER SUPPLY: The source of water supply to the property is (check appropriate boxes):

☐ Public Water Service ☐ Holding Tank ☐ Unknown

☐ Private Water Service ☐ Cistern ☐ Other _____

☐ Private Well ☐ Spring _____

☐ Shared Well ☐ Pond _____

Do you know of any current leaks, backups or other material problems with the water supply system or quality of the water? ☐ Yes
No ☐ If "Yes", please describe and indicate any repairs completed (but not longer than the past 5 years): _____
_____

Is the quantity of water sufficient for your household use? (NOTE: water usage will vary from household to household) ☐Yes ☐ No

B) SEWER SYSTEM: The nature of the sanitary sewer system servicing the property is (check appropriate boxes):

☐ Public Sewer ☐ Private Sewer ☐ Septic Tank

☐ Leach Field ☐ Aeration Tank ☐ Filtration Bed

☐ Unknown ☐ Other_____

If not a public or private sewer, date of last inspection: _____ Inspected By:_____

Do you know of **any previous or current** leaks, backups or other material problems with the sewer system servicing the property?
Yes ☐ No ☐   If "Yes", please describe and indicate any repairs completed (but not longer than the past 5 years):_____

Information on the operation and maintenance of the type of sewage system serving the property is available from the department of health or the board of health of the health district in which the property is located.

C) ROOF: Do you know of **any previous or current** leaks or other material problems with the roof or rain gutters? ☐Yes ☐No
If "Yes", please describe and indicate any repairs completed (but not longer than the past 5 years):_____
_____

D) WATER INTRUSION: Do you know of **any previous or current** water leakage, water accumulation, excess moisture or other defects to the property, including but not limited to any area below grade, basement or crawl space? ☐Yes ☐No
If "Yes", please describe and indicate any repairs completed: _____
_____

Owner's Initials _____ Date _____   Purchaser's Initials _____ Date _____

Owner's Initials _____ Date _____   Purchaser's Initials _____ Date _____

(Page 2 of 5)

Property Address_____

Do you know of any water or moisture related damage to floors, walls or ceilings as a result of flooding; moisture condensation; ice damming; sewer overflow/backup; or leaking pipes, plumbing fixtures, or appliances? ☐Yes ☐No
If "Yes", please describe and indicate any repairs completed: _____
_____

Have you ever had the property inspected for mold by a qualified inspector? ☐Yes ☐No
If "Yes", please describe and indicate whether you have an inspection report and any remediation undertaken: _____
_____

Purchaser is advised that every home contains mold. Some people are more sensitive to mold than others. If concerned about this issue, purchaser is encouraged to have a mold inspection done by a qualified inspector.

E) STRUCTURAL COMPONENTS (FOUNDATION, BASEMENT/CRAWL SPACE, FLOORS, INTERIOR AND EXTERIOR WALLS): Do you know of **any previous or current** movement, shifting, deterioration, material cracks/settling (other than visible minor cracks or blemishes) or other material problems with the foundation, basement/crawl space, floors, or interior/exterior walls?
☐Yes ☐No   If "Yes", please describe and indicate any repairs, alterations or modifications to control the cause or effect of any problem identified (but not longer than the past 5 years):_____
_____

Do you know of **any previous or current** fire or smoke damage to the property? ☐Yes ☐No
If "Yes", please describe and indicate any repairs completed: _____
_____

F) WOOD DESTROYING INSECTS/TERMITES: Do you know of **any previous/current** presence of any wood destroying insects/termites in or on the property or any existing damage to the property caused by wood destroying insects/termites?☐Yes ☐No
If "Yes", please describe and indicate any inspection or treatment (but not longer than the past 5 years):_____
_____

G) MECHANICAL SYSTEMS: Do you know of **any previous or current** problems or defects with the following existing mechanical systems? If your property does not have the mechanical system, mark N/A (Not Applicable).

	YES	NO	N/A		YES	NO	N/A
1) Electrical	☐	☐	☐	8) Water softener	☐	☐	☐
2) Plumbing (pipes)	☐	☐	☐	a. Is water softener leased?	☐	☐	☐
3) Central heating	☐	☐	☐	9) Security System	☐	☐	☐
4) Central Air conditioning	☐	☐	☐	a. Is security system leased?	☐	☐	☐
5) Sump pump	☐	☐	☐	10) Central vacuum	☐	☐	☐
6) Fireplace/chimney	☐	☐	☐	11) Built in appliances	☐	☐	☐
7) Lawn sprinkler	☐	☐	☐	12) Other mechanical systems	☐	☐	☐

If the answer to any of the above questions is "Yes", please describe and indicate any repairs to the mechanical system (but not longer than the past 5 years): _____
_____

H) PRESENCE OF HAZARDOUS MATERIALS: Do you know of the **previous or current** presence of any of the below identified hazardous materials on the property?

	Yes	No	Unknown
1) Lead-Based Paint	☐	☐	☐
2) Asbestos	☐	☐	☐
3) Urea-Formaldehyde Foam Insulation	☐	☐	☐
4) Radon Gas	☐	☐	☐
a. If "Yes", indicate level of gas if known _____			
5) Other toxic or hazardous substances	☐	☐	☐

If the answer to any of the above questions is "Yes", please describe and indicate any repairs, remediation or mitigation to the property: _____
_____

Owner's Initials _____ Date _____   Purchaser's Initials _____ Date _____
Owner's Initials _____ Date _____   Purchaser's Initials _____ Date _____

Property Address_____

I) UNDERGROUND STORAGE TANKS/WELLS: Do you know of any underground storage tanks (existing or removed), oil or natural gas wells (plugged or unplugged), or abandoned water wells on the property? ☐ Yes ☐ No
If "Yes", please describe: _____

_____

Do you know of any oil, gas, or other mineral right leases on the property? ☐ Yes ☐ No

Purchaser should exercise whatever due diligence purchaser deems necessary with respect to oil, gas, and other mineral rights. Information may be obtained from records contained within the recorder's office in the county where the property is located.

J) FLOOD PLAIN/LAKE ERIE COASTAL EROSION AREA:

	Yes	No	Unknown
Is the property located in a designated flood plain?	☐	☐	☐
Is the property or any portion of the property included in a Lake Erie Coastal Erosion Area?			

K) DRAINAGE/EROSION: Do you know of **any previous or current** flooding, drainage, settling or grading or erosion problems affecting the property? ☐ Yes ☐ No
If "Yes", please describe and indicate any repairs, modifications or alterations to the property or other attempts to control any problems (but not longer than the past 5 years):_____

_____

L) ZONING/CODE VIOLATIONS/ASSESSMENTS/HOMEOWNERS' ASSOCIATION: Do you know of any violations of building or housing codes, zoning ordinances affecting the property or any nonconforming uses of the property? ☐ Yes ☐ No
If "Yes", please describe: _____

_____

Is the structure on the property designated by any governmental authority as a historic building or as being located in an historic district? (NOTE: such designation may limit changes or improvements that may be made to the property). ☐ Yes ☐ No
If "Yes", please describe: _____

_____

Do you know of **any recent or proposed** assessments, fees or abatements, which could affect the property? ☐ Yes ☐ No
If "Yes", please describe: _____

_____

List any assessments paid in full (date/amount)_____
List any current assessments: _____ monthly fee _____ Length of payment (years _____ months _____)

Do you know of any recent or proposed rules or regulations of, or the payment of any fees or charges associated with this property, including but not limited to a Community Association, SID, CID, LID, etc. ☐ Yes ☐ No
If "Yes", please describe (amount)_____

_____

M) BOUNDARY LINES/ENCROACHMENTS/SHARED DRIVEWAY/PARTY WALLS: Do you know of any of the following conditions affecting the property?

	Yes	No		Yes	No
1) Boundary Agreement	☐	☐	4) Shared Driveway	☐	☐
2) Boundary Dispute	☐	☐	5) Party Walls	☐	☐
3) Recent Boundary Change	☐	☐	6) Encroachments From or on Adjacent Property	☐	☐

If the answer to any of the above questions is "Yes", please describe: _____

_____

N) OTHER KNOWN MATERIAL DEFECTS: The following are other known material defects in or on the property:

_____

_____

For purposes of this section, material defects would include any non-observable physical condition existing on the property that could be dangerous to anyone occupying the property or any non-observable physical condition that could inhibit a person's use of the property.

Owner's Initials _____ Date _____   Purchaser's Initials _____ Date _____
Owner's Initials _____ Date _____   Purchaser's Initials _____ Date _____

Property Address_____

CERTIFICATION OF OWNER

Owner certifies that the statements contained in this form are made in good faith and based on his/her actual knowledge as of the date signed by the Owner. Owner is advised that the information contained in this disclosure form does not limit the obligation of the owner to disclose an item of information that is required by any other statute or law or that may exist to preclude fraud, either by misrepresentation, concealment or nondisclosure in a transaction involving the transfer of residential real estate.

OWNER: _____   DATE: _____

OWNER: _____   DATE: _____

RECEIPT AND ACKNOWLEDGEMENT OF POTENTIAL PURCHASERS

Potential purchasers are advised that the owner has no obligation to update this form but may do so according to Revised Code Section 5302.30(G). Pursuant to Ohio Revised Code Section 5302.30(K), if this form is not provided to you prior to the time you enter into a purchase contract for the property, you may rescind the purchase contract by delivering a signed and dated document of rescission to Owner or Owner's agent, provided the document of rescission is delivered prior to all three of the following dates: 1) the date of closing; 2) 30 days after the Owner accepted your offer; and 3) within 3 business days following your receipt or your agent's receipt of this form or an amendment of this form.

Owner makes no representations with respect to any offsite conditions. Purchaser should exercise whatever due diligence purchaser deems necessary with respect to offsite issues that may affect purchaser's decision to purchase the property.

Purchaser should exercise whatever due diligence purchaser deems necessary with respect to Ohio's Sex Offender Registration and Notification Law (commonly referred to as "Megan's Law"). This law requires the local Sheriff to provide written notice to neighbors if a sex offender resides or intends to reside in the area. The notice provided by the Sheriff is a public record and is open to inspection under Ohio's Public Records Law. If concerned about this issue, purchaser assumes responsibility to obtain information from the Sheriff's office regarding the notices they have provided pursuant to Megan's Law.

Purchaser should exercise whatever due diligence purchaser deems necessary with respect to abandoned underground mines. If concerned about this issue, purchaser assumes responsibility to obtain information from the Ohio Department of Natural Resources. The Department maintains an online map of known abandoned underground mines on their website at www.dnr.state.oh.us.

I/WE ACKNOWLEDGE RECEIPT OF A COPY OF THIS DISCLOSURE FORM AND UNDERSTAND THAT THE STATEMENTS ARE MADE BASED ON THE OWNERS ACTUAL KNOWLEDGE AS OF THE DATE SIGNED BY THE OWNER.

My/Our Signature below does not constitute approval of any disclosed condition as represented herein by the owner.

PURCHASER: _____   DATE: _____

PURCHASER: _____   DATE: _____

(Page 5 of 5)

Lead-Based Paint Disclosure Regulations

- Federal laws took effect March 1996. Regulated by EPA and HUD.

- Sellers and lessors of properties built before 1978 *must* disclose their actual knowledge of lead-based paint hazards.

- A real estate agent has the responsibility to ensure that the seller or lessor satisfies the disclosure obligations.

- Buyer agents who receive *all* their compensation from the purchaser are exempt.

- At the time of signing the listing, the agent must perform all of the following steps:

    1. Determine when the home was built

    2. Advise the seller of his obligations under the Lead-Based Paint Disclosure

    3. Obtain from seller any information related to the presence of lead-based paint

    4. Have the seller complete and sign the disclosure form

EPA and HUD regulations issued to implement these disclosures are summarized as follows:

1. Sellers and landlords must disclose any known lead-based paint hazard in homes, and must give buyers and tenants any reports available from prior lead tests.

2. Sellers and landlords must give buyers and renters a pamphlet about how to protect families from lead in homes.

3. Homebuyers have a 10-day period (or other mutually agreed upon time) to conduct a lead paint inspection or risk assessment at their own expense, if desired.

4. Sellers, landlords, and real estate agents must include certain language in sales contracts and/or leasing agreements to ensure that disclosure and notification actually take place. This has been included in most board real estate contracts.

According to HUD, real estate agents must comply with the law if the seller or landlord fails to do so, but the agent is not responsible if the owner conceals information or fails to disclose it. The penalty for failure to disclose lead hazards is a fine of up to $10,000 and up to one year in jail, plus treble damages. The written disclosure and pamphlet must be given *prior to* a seller accepting a buyer's written offer to purchase, or *prior to* a landlord accepting a tenant's offer to rent. (Remodelers must also give the pamphlet, but not the form.)

Properties exempt from lead paint disclosure rules include: Zero-bedroom units, such as lofts or dormitories; leases for less than 100 days; housing exclusively for the elderly; housing for the disabled (unless children live there); rental units that have been inspected and found to be lead-free; and houses sold by foreclosure.

Disclosure of Information on Lead-Based Paint and/or Lead-Based Paint Hazards

Lead Warning Statement

Every purchaser of any interest in residential real property on which a residential dwelling was built prior to 1978 is notified that such property may present exposure to lead from lead-based paint that may place young children at risk of developing lead poisoning. Lead poisoning in young children may produce permanent neurological damage, including learning disabilities, reduced intelligence quotient, behavioral problems, and impaired memory. Lead poisoning also poses a particular risk to pregnant women. The seller of any interest in residential real property is required to provide the buyer with any information on lead-based paint hazards from risk assessments or inspections in the seller's possession and notify the buyer of any known lead-based paint hazards. A risk assessment or inspection for possible lead-based paint hazards is recommended prior to purchase.

Seller's Disclosure

(a) Presence of lead-based paint and/or lead-based paint hazards (check (i) or (ii) below):

  (i) _____ Known lead-based paint and/or lead-based paint hazards are present in the housing (explain).

  _____

  (ii) _____ Seller has no knowledge of lead-based paint and/or lead-based paint hazards in the housing.

(b) Records and reports available to the seller (check (i) or (ii) below):

  (i) _____ Seller has provided the purchaser with all available records and reports pertaining to lead-based paint and/or lead-based paint hazards in the housing (list documents below).

  _____

  (ii) _____ Seller has no reports or records pertaining to lead-based paint and/or lead-based paint hazards in the housing.

Purchaser's Acknowledgment (initial)

(c) _____ Purchaser has received copies of all information listed above.

(d) _____ Purchaser has received the pamphlet *Protect Your Family from Lead in Your Home.*

(e) Purchaser has (check (i) or (ii) below):

  (i) _____ received a 10-day opportunity (or mutually agreed upon period) to conduct a risk assessment or inspection for the presence of lead-based paint and/or lead-based paint hazards; or

  (ii) _____ waived the opportunity to conduct a risk assessment or inspection for the presence of lead-based paint and/or lead-based paint hazards.

Agent's Acknowledgment (initial)

(f) _____ Agent has informed the seller of the seller's obligations under 42 U.S.C. 4852(d) and is aware of his/her responsibility to ensure compliance.

Certification of Accuracy

The following parties have reviewed the information above and certify, to the best of their knowledge, that the information they have provided is true and accurate.

Seller	Date	Seller	Date
Purchaser	Date	Purchaser	Date
Agent	Date	Agent	Date

Glossary

Agency Relationship Under the common law, this relationship is defined as:

1. Agency is the fiduciary relationship that results from the manifestation of consent by one person to another that the other shall act on his behalf and subject to his control, and consent by the other so to act.

2. The one for whom action is taken is the principal.

3. The one who is to act is the agent.

In a real estate transaction, the agency relationship is formed between the brokerage firm (including all their licensees) and the principal.

Alternative MLS See **MLS PLUS**.

Apparent Agency (also referred to as **Obstensbile Agency**) When someone without any authority (either actual or implied) holds himself out as an agent working for a principle. If the principle takes no action to stop the apparent agent; then the principle will himself be "estopped" from asserting that the apparent agent really is not his agent.

Blanket Unilateral Offer of Subagency An automatic offer that is made by a listing agent to all other members of the Multiple Listing Service (MLS) when he submits his seller's listing to a traditional MLS; the offer is accepted whenever an agent shows the listed property without rejecting the offer. (No longer used in Ohio.)

Buyer Agency The agency relationship that exists between a buyer principal and the buyer's agent.

Buyer Agency Exclusively The practice of representing only the buyer and never the seller in a transaction.

Buyer's Agent A real estate agent who is employed by and represents only the buyer in a real estate transaction, regardless of whether the commission is paid by the buyer or by the seller, or through a commission split with the listing agent.

Client A buyer or seller represented by an agent who is subject to that buyer's or seller's control; also called a **principal**.

Contingent Fee Any fee that is conditional upon some event occurring, usually a closing.

Cooperating Agent See **Selling Agent**.

Customer A buyer who is working with an agent who represents the seller; also the seller of unlisted property that is being sold to a buyer represented by a buyer's agent.

Disclosed Dual Agency A dual agency relationship where the brokerage firm, by written or oral means, discloses and receives informed consent from both the buyer and the seller to act in a dual agency capacity.

Disclosed Dual Agent A real estate agent who has received informed consent from both a buyer and seller in the same transaction to act in a dual agency capacity.

Dual Agency An agency relationship where the brokerage firm represents both the buyer and the seller in the same transaction to act in a dual agency capacity.

Facilitator A person who assists the parties to a potential real estate transaction in communication, interposition, and negotiation to reach agreement between or among them, without being an advocate for the interests of any party except the mutual interest of all parties to reach agreement. Also known as an **intermediary**. (Not recognized in Ohio.)

Fiduciary Duties Duties owed by an agent to his principal (**ACCOLD**):

1. **Accounting** – Acknowledges that all money received in the agency relationship belongs to the principal, not the agent. The agent has the duty to strictly account for any amounts received in a transaction on behalf of the principal.

2. **Confidentiality**- Agents must not reveal confidential information of a client.

3. **Care (Reasonable Care and Skill)** – Must be used by an agent at all times when acting on behalf of a client. Agents are seen as trusted professionals and experts, and as such, are held to a minimum standard of competence. Expertise should never be claimed in areas where one does not have special training, and agents must be careful never to engage in the unauthorized practice of law.

4. **Obedience** – Agents must follow all legal directions of the principal, obey the restrictions of the agency relationship, and not stray beyond scope of authority.

5. **Loyalty** – Agents must put the principal's best interests above all others, including the agent's own.

6. **Disclosure** – An agent is obligated to disclose to his principal all relevant and material information, unless obtained through a previous fiduciary relationship, that the agent knows and that pertains to the scope of the agency. Duties of disclosure include: True property value, all offers to purchase, identity of the prospective buyer, buyer's financial condition, any relationship between the buyer and the broker, and any commission splitting arrangements with other brokers.

Implied Agency Any agency relationship that is indicated by the words and/or actions of the agent rather than by written agreement; also called **accidental** or **undisclosed agency**.

Informed Consent A person's agreement to allow something to happen that is based on a full disclosure of facts needed to make the decision intelligently, e.g., knowledge of liability involved, alternatives.

In-Company Sale A sale in which one real estate brokerage company acts as both the listing and selling agent.

Intermediary *See* **Facilitator**.

Listing Agent An agent of the seller who markets that seller's property, usually exclusively, and represents the seller during the sale and closing of the property. Also known as **seller's agent**.

Multiple Listing Service (MLS) An organized system created to disseminate information about listed properties and through which members offer cooperation and compensation to their participants; usually a committee of a Board or a corporation owned by a Board.

MLS PLUS MLS policy that allows listing agents to indicate the fee they will pay a buyer's agent as well as the fee they will pay to a subagent upon a successful closing. An offer of subagency is mandatory. Also known as **alternative MLS**, but is *not* in all markets.

Participating Agent *See* **Selling Agent**.

Procuring Cause The proximate cause originating a series of events that, without break in their continuity, results in the accomplishment of the objective. A real estate broker will be regarded as the "procuring cause" of a sale, so as to be entitled to commission, if the broker's efforts are the foundation on which the negotiations resulting in a sale are begun.

Seller's Agent A real estate agent who is employed by and represents only the seller in a real estate transaction. Also known as **listing agent**.

Selling Agent Any agent who sells a property; she may be the subagent or listing agent of the seller, or a buyer's agent, or a dual agent. Also called a **cooperating agent**, or **participating agent**.

Seller Agency The agency relationship that exists between a seller principal and the seller's agent.

Seller Agency And Buyer Agency with Disclosed Dual Agency for In-Company Sales The practice of representing the party you are working with (either buyer or seller) and becoming a disclosed dual agent for in-company sales.

Seller Agency Exclusively The practice of representing only the seller and never the buyer in a transaction.

Single Agency The practice of representing either the buyer or the seller, but never both, in the same transaction.

Split Agency A situation in which one agent represents the buyer and another agent from the same real estate brokerage represents the seller. The broker and all management-level employees are dual agents of both buyer and seller. The broker may also appoint a specific agent to represent the seller and another specific agent (from the same firm) to represent the buyer. Also known as **in-company transaction**.

Subagent An agent employed to act for another agent in performing functions undertaken for a principal, who owes the same duties and responsibilities to the principal as the principal's agent. Correspondingly, the subagent can create the same liabilities for the agent and principal that the agent can create for the principal himself.

Subagency Optional MLS MLS in which listing agents must offer cooperation but don't automatically offer subagency; the offer of compensation may be to buyer's agents, subagents and/or listing agents; subagency may be offered.

Undisclosed Dual Agency A dual agency relationship that occurs when a listing agent or subagent acts or speaks as though he also represents the buyer but without either written or oral disclosure. Conversely, dual agency also occurs when an agent of the buyer acts or speaks as if he also represents the seller.

Sample Law Exams

LAW EXAM ONE

1. **Ohio real estate educational requirements state that all new licensees must take**

   a. 40 hours of real estate principles and practices; 40 hours of real estate law; 20 hours of real estate appraisal; and 20 hours of real estate finance at an institution of higher education.

   b. a 20-hour post-licensing course within one year of passing the state exam.

   c. 30 hours of continuing education courses, unless you get a special "senior waiver" that permits you to take only 9 hours.

   d. All of the above

2. **If a real estate licensee fails to take all the required courses for continuing education, his license is**

   a. automatically suspended

   b. automatically revoked

   c. held on deposit until fulfillment of the courses

   d. held in escrow until notified by his local board

3. **Under Ohio Complaint Procedures, when a complaint is filed by the Ohio Civil Rights Commission, upon request, a complaint hearing may be heard by which of the following?**

   a. Hearing Examiner

   b. Superintendent of Real Estate

   c. Ohio Real Estate Commission

   d. Ohio Civil Rights Commission

4. **Which is the correct appeal process regarding complaint hearings under Ohio law?**

   a. Superintendent, Ohio Civil Rights Commission, Common Pleas Court

   b. Hearing Examiner, Ohio Real Estate Commission, Common Pleas Court

   c. Hearing Examiner, Superintendent of Real Estate, Ohio Real Estate Commission, Common Pleas Court

   d. Hearing Examiner, Superintendent of Real Estate, Ohio Real Estate Commission

5. **Which of the following continuing education courses must be taken by Ohio real estate salespersons and brokers who are younger than 70 years of age?**

   a. 30 hours of continuing education, of which 3 hours must include civil rights

   b. 30 hours of continuing education, of which 3 hours must include civil rights, 3 hours must include a core law course, and 3 hours of Canons of Ethics, as long as they are approved by the Ohio Division of Real Estate

   c. 30 hours of any continuing education courses, as long as they are approved by the Ohio Real Estate Division

   d. 30 hours of real estate finance and appraisal, as long as the agent/broker are licensed after January 1, 1990

6. **A real estate sales licensee may transfer her license in which of the following time periods?**

    a. in any month that she chooses to do so

    b. in any month, except the month of december, unless in a case of undue hardship

    c. only at the end of the year when the continuation of business form is filed by the broker

    d. none of the above

7. **Under Ohio license law, the broker's name and advertising must be displayed in which of the following ways?**

    a. larger than that of the salesperson

    b. at least in equal prominence with that of the salesperson

    c. the broker's name only must appear

    d. size in advertising is discretionary by the broker and negotiated with the salesperson

8. **When a judgment is satisfied out of the Ohio Real Estate Recovery Fund against a licensee, which of the following will happen to the licensee?**

    a. The licensee can never practice real estate in the state of Ohio.

    b. The licensee's license is automatically. suspended for a period of three years.

    c. The licensee's license is automatically suspended until such monies are paid back into the Real Estate Recovery Fund, plus interest.

    d. none of the above

9. **It is the duty of which of the following to notify real estate agents of any changes in the law pertaining to discrimination in real estate sales?**

    a. Ohio Civil Rights Commission

    b. Ohio Real Estate Commission

    c. local real estate board

    d. their attorney, who represents the broker

10. **In stating the expiration of a listing contract, the proper language would be:**

    a. "This listing contract shall expire in 90 days."

    b. "This listing contract shall expire in 90 days from the signing hereof."

    c. "This listing contract shall expire 90 days from the signing hereof, that day being December 31, 2001 at 12:00 p.m."

    d. none of the above

11. **A hearing will result with regard to a complaint at the discretion of the**

    a. Superintendent of Real Estate.

    b. complainant only.

    c. licensee only.

    d. Ohio Real Estate Commission.

12. **An Ohio real estate salesperson can receive compensation from which of the following parties with regard to real estate sales?**

    a. from any broker as long as the salesperson receives it from a cooperating broker

    b. it is up to the listing broker

    c. from any broker who has the same franchise name as his broker

    d. only from his broker

13. **After the purchaser signs the sales contract, the salesperson must do which of the following?**

    a. keep the original contract for his files and give the purchaser a copy the following day

    b. give the purchaser a copy immediately

    c. mail the purchaser a copy of the contract after the statutory 3-day cooling off period has expired

    d. none of the above

14. **Which of the following applies to the real estate salesperson's license?**

    a. The salesperson's license belongs to the agent, yet must be on file, available upon request, in the broker's office.

    b. The salesperson's license must be registered within 45 days of issuance.

    c. The salesperson's license must be displayed on the wall next to the broker's license and the Equal Housing Opportunity Poster.

    d. A and B only

15. **When a real estate sales agent receives an earnest money deposit, that money must be**

   a. deposited in the agent's own trust account until the agent has time to deposit the money into the broker's trust account.

   b. deposited according to the terms of the contract.

   c. held in the broker's safe until after the transaction is consummated.

   d. none of the above

16. **Under Ohio Real Estate License Law, a real estate sales agent who is drafted into the armed services may do which of the following?**

   a. put his license on deposit until the next renewal date after his discharge

   b. request the Ohio real estate commission to suspend his license until discharged from the armed services

   c. take no action since he is completely protected under the veteran's administration act

   d. retake the Ohio Real Estate Law class after discharge from the armed services

17. **Under Ohio License Law, which of the following parties should teach Ohio Real Estate Law wherever feasible?**

   a. a local real estate attorney

   b. a staff member of the Ohio civil rights commission

   c. a faculty member of an accredited law school

   d. any licensed broker with 10 years or more experience

18. **A real estate salesperson may be licensed with and have her license held by**

   a. a limited real estate broker.

   b. a real estate broker.

   c. other real estate salespersons.

   d. all of the above

19. **Wherever feasible, classroom instruction given in real estate law with regard to fair housing and civil rights law in preparation for taking the Ohio Sales or Broker's examinations should be taught by**

   a. a member of the faculty of an accredited law school.

   b. local real estate attorneys.

   c. someone from the Ohio Civil Rights Commission.

   d. any licensed broker with 10 years, or more , of experience.

20. **To take the Ohio real estate sales license examination, you must**

   a. be honest, truthful, and of good reputation.

   b. be at least 18 years of age.

   c. not have committed a felony or crime of moral turpitude, or have violated any civil rights law (felony is "OK" on a case-by-case basis).

   d. all of the above

21. **The definition of a real estate broker includes any person, partnership, association, or corporation who**

   a. offers, attempts, or agrees to negotiate the sale, exchange, purchase, rental, or leasing of any real estate.

   b. brings the buyer and seller together for a fee, commission, or other valuable consideration.

   c. directs or assists in the procuring of prospects for the negotiation of any transaction, other than mortgage financing, which is calculated to result in a sale, exchange, leasing, or rental of real estate.

   d. all of the above

22. **The Ohio Real Estate Commission must**

   a. include five licensed brokers, all of whom are appointed by the Governor.

   b. include five commissioners, four of whom must be licensed brokers, with one member representing the public, all of whom are appointed by the Governor.

   c. the number of commissioners changes each year with the election of the Governor.

   d. none of the above

23. **It is the duty of the Ohio Real Estate Commission to**
    a. adopt canons of ethics for the real estate industry.
    b. hear appeals with regard to complaints received by the superintendent of real estate.
    c. notify licensees of changes in state and federal civil rights laws pertaining to real estate.
    d. all of the above

24. **The Superintendent of Real Estate is appointed by the**
    a. Director of Commerce.
    b. Ohio Real Estate Commission.
    c. Governor.
    d. Superintendent Election Committee.

25. **Upon the death of a licensed broker, or the revocation or suspension of his license, and with no other licensed broker within the entity, upon proper application, an ancillary trustee shall be appointed to conclude the business transactions of the deceased, revoked or suspended broker by the**
    a. Superintendent of Real Estate (in the event of death with approval of the probate court).
    b. Ohio Real Estate Commission.
    c. Director of Commerce.
    d. attorney for the estate.

26. **Upon the death of a licensed broker, or the revocation or suspension of his license, and there is no other licensed broker within the business entity, the party who may be appointed to conclude the business transactions of the deceased, revoked, or suspended broker, would be**
    a. the Ohio Real Estate Commission.
    b. the deceased broker's attorney.
    c. an ancillary trustee.
    d. the Governor of the state of Ohio.

27. **Under Ohio real estate law, there are what types of hearings available to a complainant and a licensee?**
    a. informal mediation hearing only
    b. formal hearing only
    c. informal and formal mediation hearings, but informal only if both parties agree
    d. formal and informal mediation hearing if the complainant agrees

28. **If a formal hearing is to be held with regard to a complaint filed against a real estate agent, the initial hearing shall be heard by**
    a. an investigator from the Hearing and Audit Section of the Division of Real Estate.
    b. a hearing examiner.
    c. a board of arbitrators appointed by the Ohio Real Estate Commission.
    d. the Ohio Real Estate Commission.

29. **Whenever an application fee or transfer fee is paid to the state of Ohio with regard to real estate agents or brokers, the amount that shall be paid to the research and education fund is**
    a. dependent on the current balance in the fund.
    b. dependent on the size of the brokerage company.
    c. $1.00.
    d. none of the above

30. **The amount of money that must be sent to the Ohio Division of Real Estate with the application to take the Ohio real estate sales examination is**
    a. $60.00.
    b. $49.00 refundable fee upon passing.
    c. $39.00.
    d. dependent on the number of licensees taking the examination.

31. **Carla signs a two-year lease for a luxury apartment. In the lease, it states that the security deposit is non-refundable. When the lease ends, what will happen to the security deposit?**
    a. the landlord gets to keep it
    b. Carla gets it back
    c. it has to stay in a non-interest bearing account
    d. it carries over to the next tenant

32. *In Ohio, how much interest does the owner give the tenant when the security deposit exceeds the amount of the rent?*

    a. 10%
    b. 6%
    c. 5%
    d. 7%

33. *Mearle moved out of his apartment. 20 days later, he gets a notice that his security deposit was kept to pay the cleaners who washed the walls and shampooed the carpet. How much needed to be returned to Mearle?*

    a. all of it
    b. half of it
    c. three quarters
    d. none of it

34. *A prospective tenant writes a check for a security deposit but says that it isn't good for 5 more days. The property manager should*

    a. not accept the check
    b. accept the check and wait to deposit it.
    c. ask for additional asset to hold until the check is good
    d. call the police because the tenant is trying to pass a bad check

35. *Sharon rents an apartment for $550 a month and makes a $700 security deposit. A family problem arises and she moves home to take care of it after only living in her apartment for 4 months. How much interest does the landlord have to give her for the amount above the monthly rent?*

    a. none
    b. 5%
    c. 1.67%
    d. 3%

LAW EXAM TWO

1. **A salesperson may operate from any office that the salesperson's broker designates, provided**
   a. the broker is duly licensed.
   b. the salesperson notified the board.
   c. the license states the proper address.
   d. all of the above

2. **When a party has been damaged through the negligence of a real estate agent or broker, and there are no funds available from which to seek compensation, the party may turn to the state of Ohio and ask that money be paid from**
   a. the Real Estate Research Fund.
   b. the Ohio Real Estate Commission.
   c. the Real Estate Recovery Fund.
   d. none of the above

3. **A party who has been damaged by the negligence of a real estate agent or broker may receive compensation from the Real Estate Recovery Fund if**
   a. he has diligently pursued his remedies against all judgment debtors and all other persons liable to him.
   b. there are punitive damages being awarded with regard to this judgment.
   c. he has waived his appeal process.
   d. none of the above

4. **The maximum amount for which the Real Estate Recovery Fund may pay money out to a party who has been damaged through the negligence of a licensee or broker is**
   a. $4,000 per transaction.
   b. $40,000 per transaction.
   c. $40,000 per licensee.
   d. dependent on the number of real estate agents within each broker's entity.

5. **Ohio real estate license laws require that the license of a real estate broker be:**
   a. made available immediately upon request by Ohio Real Estate Commission.
   b. prominently displayed in the office or place of business of the broker next to the Equal Housing Opportunity poster.
   c. The statute is not real clear on this.
   d. The Ohio Real Estate Commission holds all brokers' licenses.

6. **The license of each real estate salesperson issued belongs to**
   a. the real estate licensee.
   b. their real estate broker.
   c. the Ohio Division of Real Estate.
   d. none of the above

7. **When a salesperson wishes to change brokers, because the broker's license is suspended or revoked, she must**
   a. notify, in writing, the Ohio Division of Real Estate and pay the appropriate fee.
   b. tell the broker only, because her license belongs to him.
   c. file application within 30 days of transfer.
   d. do nothing, as her new broker will register her on the continuation form filed before December 31st of each ensuing year.

8. **All real estate licensees shall, on or before their third birthday following the year of issurance,**
   a. renew their license by filing a Certificate of Renewal on a form prescribed by the Superintendent of Real Estate, otherwise, their licensed shall be suspended.
   b. file for recertification with the Ohio Division of Real Estate.
   c. nothing, as their licenses are automatically renewed every two years.
   d. they need not do anything.

9. **During periods of rising interest rates, which clause in a mortgage is most beneficial to the mortgagor if the loan is one with an adjustable rate?**

   a. Alliteration

   b. Acceleration

   c. Prepayment

   d. Escalator

10. **Upon passing the state examination, which of the following things must new licensees do?**

    a. record their licensed at the county recorder's office

    b. register their licensed in the clerk of courts where the broker's principal place of business is

    c. have their licensed notarized and filed with the Ohio Division of Real Estate

    d. none of the above

11. **Any licensee or broker who is found guilty as to any violation of Chapter 4735.18 of the Ohio Revised Code (Causes for Suspension or Revocation of License) may subject themselves to which of the following disciplinary actions?**

    a. civil action

    b. criminal action

    c. suspension or revocation of license by the Ohio Real Estate Commission

    d. all of the above

12. **It is required by Ohio Real Estate Law that a broker must keep complete and accurate records of all transactions**

    a. at least one year after the closing of the transaction.

    b. for a period of three years.

    c. for as long as he holds tax records.

    d. none of the above

13. **A real estate agent may subject himself to disciplinary action if he fails to give a party to a transaction a copy of any signed documents**

    a. immediately upon their signing.

    b. within 24 hours.

    c. within the statutory 3-day cooling off period.

    d. none of the above

14. **The real estate broker or salesperson needs to have**

    a. little understanding of law because competent attorneys are available.

    b. a broad understanding of law and how it affects real estate.

    c. legal experience as a practicing attorney.

    d. an in-depth understanding of constitutional law.

15. **A broker advertised a listed property, stating only the address, no price, and "for details call 412-281-8030." A sale results. Which of the following is a TRUE statement?**

    a. the broker cannot collect commission

    b. the broker is guilty of a misdemeanor

    c. the broker's license may be suspended or revoked because the advertisement does not state that the broker is a licensed real estate broker

    d. the buyer has a cause of action against the broker

16. **The Ohio Real Estate Commission is required, by law, to**

    a. promulgate Canons of Ethics for the real estate industry.

    b. administer the Education and Research fund.

    c. direct the Superintendent on the content, scheduling, instruction, and offerings of real estate courses for real estate salesperson and broker educational requirements.

    d. all of the above

17. **A broker and two of his more experienced salespersons desire to form a partnership to engage in the business of real estate. The broker is to have a 40% interest, with each salesperson owning 30%. Which of the following is correct?**
    a. They can form the partnership as desired.
    b. They cannot form the partnership, as each must have equal interest.
    c. They cannot form the partnership; two of the parties are not licensed as brokers.
    d. They may form the partnership since all parties are licensed as salespersons and brokers.

18. **Since violations of the license law are detrimental to the public and licensees generally, it is your duty to:**
    a. Keep quiet about them
    b. Inform the newspapers so they may be exposed
    c. Notify the Division of Real Estate
    d. Notify the local real estate board

19. **A broker's license is revoked for one year. His two salespersons:**
    a. Must remain on inactive status the balance of the license year
    b. Would lose their licenses for one year
    c. May, upon proper application, transfer to another broker
    d. May continue to operate the broker's business

20. **A definite expiration time and date in a listing agreement is required by:**
    a. The local real estate board
    b. Ohio law
    c. The Ohio Real Estate Commission
    d. The Civil Rights Commission

21. **Real estate agency advertising must be in the name of the:**
    a. Seller
    b. Licensed broker
    c. Sales associate who obtains the listing
    d. Real estate sales associate on the premises

22. **If a license is issued on October 1, it will expire**
    a. one year from the date of issuance.
    b. six months from the date of issuance.
    c. on the licensee's first birthday.
    d. none of the above

23. **The Superintendent of Real Estate decides whether**
    a. there will be an informal mediation hearing of a complaint.
    b. there will be a formal hearing of a complaint.
    c. there will be no hearing of a complaint.
    d. both b and c

24. **Educational loans may be awarded, provided they are**
    a. applied for when need is shown.
    b. not in excess of $800.
    c. co-signed by the sponsoring broker as guarantor of the loan.
    d. all of the above

25. **Which of the following can a real estate licensee prepare for another broker for a fee?**
    a. the contract for sale
    b. a deed
    c. a land contract
    d. none of the above because that would be unauthorized practice of law

26. **Upon initial hearing of a complaint, a real estate licensee is subject to which of these?**
    a. His license is automatically suspended.
    b. His license is automatically revoked.
    c. His license will not be suspended or revoked until the Ohio Real Estate Commission also conducts a hearing.
    d. None of the above

27. **The Ohio real estate license laws were passed**
    a. for political reasons only.
    b. to protect the public.
    c. to protect new salespersons.
    d. to raise revenues for the Real Estate Education fund.

28. **A hearing resulting from a complaint shall be heard by**
    a. the Ohio Real Estate Commission.
    b. the Superintendent of Real Estate.
    c. a hearing examiner.
    d. the investigator from the Hearing and Audit Section.

29. **A salesperson may begin the practice of real estate**
    a. as soon as she completes his 10-hour post-licensing requirement.
    b. as soon as her license is registered.
    c. as soon as her license is issued.
    d. upon passing the exam.

30. **Under Ohio Real Estate Law, if you have knowledge of a violation of the Real Estate License Law under Chapter 4735.18 of the Ohio Revised Code (Causes for Suspension or Revocation of License), you must**
    a. notify your local real estate board.
    b. notify the Ohio Civil Rights Commission.
    c. notify the Ohio Division of Real Estate.
    d. all of the above

31. **Andy is selling his apartment building of ten residential units that brings in $750 per unit per month. If the closing is on October 10th, how much will the buyer receive from the seller if the owner charged each unit dweller a $700 security deposit?**
    a. $12,080.65
    b. $5,280.64
    c. $7,000
    d. $750

32. **Which of the following must be provided to a tenant within 30 days of terminating tenancy?**
    a. copy of the lease
    b. Consumer Guide to Agency
    c. security deposit and/or list of items that deducted from the security deposit
    d. bill for carpet cleaning

33. **Of the following, which item can be deducted from the security deposit?**
    a. carpet cleaning
    b. cost to paint the walls
    c. water damage caused by tenant negligence
    d. replacement of old appliances

34. **Charlotte rented an apartment from Mr. Spencer. Charlotte is obligated to give the landlord $600 for rent. She was charged a $1,000 security deposit. What must the landlord give the tenant (besides possession)?**
    a. nothing
    b. a receipt
    c. a copy of the lease
    d. 5% interest per anum on the difference between $600 and $1,000.

35. **Ben is leasing his building for use as a candy factory. In the lease, Cody, the tenant, did not notice the words "non-refundable" next to the amount of deposit of $2,000. When the lease ends two years later, Cody decides not to make candy and terminates the lease. What will happen to the security deposit of $2,000?**
    a. Cody gets it back within 30 days.
    b. Cody gets it back, plus interest, because his rent was only $1,200.
    c. Cody gets it back because of the Landlord and Tenants Act.
    d. Cody will never get his deposit back.

NOTES

NOTES

Answer Key – Law Exam One

1.	D
2.	A
3.	C
4.	C
5.	B
6.	A
7.	B
8.	C
9.	B
10.	C
11.	A
12.	D
13.	B
14.	A
15.	B
16.	A
17.	C
18.	B
19.	C
20.	D
21.	D
22.	B
23.	D
24.	A
25.	A
26.	C
27.	C
28.	B
29.	C
30.	A
31.	B
32.	C
33.	A
34.	A
35.	A

Answer Key – Law Exam Two

1.	A
2.	C
3.	A
4.	C
5.	B
6.	A
7.	A
8.	A
9.	D
10.	D
11.	D
12.	B
13.	A
14.	B
15.	C
16.	D
17.	C
18.	C
19.	C
20.	B
21.	B
22.	C
23.	D
24.	D
25.	D
26.	C
27.	B
28.	C
29.	C
30.	C
31.	A
32.	C
33.	C
34.	D
35.	D